# FUNDAMENTALS OF LEGAL RESEARCH

NINTH EDITION

and

# LEGAL RESEARCH ILLUSTRATED

NINTH EDITION

By

**STEVEN M. BARKAN**

Director of Library and Information Services and Professor of Law
University of Wisconsin Law School

**ROY M. MERSKY**

Late Harry M. Reasoner Regents Chair in Law and Director of Research
The Jamail Center for Legal Research, Tarlton Law Library
University of Texas School of Law

**DONALD J. DUNN**

Late Dean and Professor of Law
University of LaVerne College of Law

## ASSIGNMENTS

**MARY ANN NELSON, EDITOR**

Executive Law Librarian
University of Iowa Law Library

FOUNDATION PRESS
2009

THOMSON REUTERS™

© 2009 By THOMSON REUTERS/FOUNDATION PRESS
195 Broadway, 9th Floor
New York, NY 10007
Phone Toll Free 1–877–888–1330
Fax (212) 367–6799
foundation–press.com
Printed in the United States of America

ISBN 978–1–59941–349–5

TO THE STUDENT:

Mastering the many nuances of legal research requires exercising the skills described in *Fundamentals of Legal Research* (9th ed.) or *Legal Research Illustrated* (9th ed.). This is the purpose of this assignment book.

We have provided numerous types of problems to introduce many aspects of legal research. The chapters in this assignment book correspond to the chapters of *Fundamentals of Legal Research* and *Legal Research Illustrated*.

Some problems specifically direct you to a particular source. Other problems require you to choose a specific title within a series or multivolume work. Another group of problems is less directive as to the resource that may answer the question. This variety of assignments is provided to exercise two skills: an ability to choose among different approaches to resolving a legal problem and an ability to glean the most information when limited to a particular resource.

Keep in mind four criteria when choosing among resources. First, what is the scope of a particular title? Does this title exclusively cover the information you desire or will you have to deal with superfluous information in order to answer the problem? Second, how is a particular title arranged? Does the title provide a "How to Use" guide? Third, how is the title you have chosen to answer the question indexed? Is there a combination of tables and indexes that provide a comprehensive approach to the information in the title or is access limited? Finally, how current is the information provided in the title? Do you need current information to answer the question? How is the information updated – through cumulative supplements, pocket parts, replacement volumes, looseleaf pages, or new editions? Is the indexing appropriately current to the form of updating?

Although these issues appear generic, their application to a problem can aid you as you pursue the course of study in *Fundamentals* or *Legal Research Illustrated* and the assignment book. If you are not comfortable in using certain types of legal materials following your readings and classroom lectures, apply the scope, arrangement, index, and update strategy. This analysis is particularly useful having the book(s) in hand. A few moments in the library using this approach can save hours of frustration.

We have provided many duplicate types of problems so your classmates will not have to share one particular book. Although you may not be doing the same problems, the questions are designed to be balanced and to exercise identical or similar skills. There are no "trick questions." If you find you are laboring over a particular question longer than fifteen minutes, seek assistance from your instructor or librarian. Maintain a detailed record of your research strategy (or pathfinder). When you encounter obstacles in your research, reviewing the pathfinder with an instructor or librarian can facilitate clarifying your confusion.

Problem solving in the legal profession involves gathering the operative facts, identifying the legal issues, researching the legal issues, and resolving the legal issues through effective writing by applying the law to the factual setting. Each of these steps builds upon the other. Successful lawyering requires analysis and research. Your first year of law school introduces each step. Equal attention must be given to each process component if you are to be successful as a lawyer. Many times poor analysis or confused writing is the result of ineffectual research. Diligence in using these assignments in conjunction with *Fundamentals of Legal Research* or *Legal Research Illustrated* provides you with a sound foundation in the legal process.

Mary Ann Nelson
University of Iowa
School of Law

Iowa City, Iowa
February 2009

# TABLE OF CONTENTS

TO THE STUDENT iii

**Chapter:**

Refers to chapters in *Fundamentals of Legal Research* (9th ed.)
and *Legal Research Illustrated* [*L.R.I.*] (9th ed.)

| | | |
|---|---|---|
| 5. | Federal Court Reports | 1 |
| 6. | State Court Reports and the National Reporter System | 17 |
| 7. | Digests for Court Reports | 31 |
| 8. | Constitutional Law | 65 |
| 9. | Federal Legislation | 82 |
| 10. | Federal Legislative Histories | 104 |
| 11. | State and Municipal Legislation [State Legislation in *L.R.I.*] | 117 |
| 12. | Court Rules and Procedures | 129 |
| 13. | Administrative Law | 138 |
| 14. | Looseleaf Services | 142 |
| 15. | Citators | 149 |
| 16. | Legal Encyclopedias | 176 |
| 17. | American Law Reports | 186 |
| 18. | Legal Periodicals and Indexes | 218 |
| 19. | Treatises, Restatements, Uniform Laws, and Model Acts | 229 |
| 20. | Practice Materials and other Resources [No Assignments] | |
| 21. | International Law | 238 |
| 22. | Legal Research in the United Kingdom [Not in *L.R.I.*] | 255 |
| 23. | Electronic Legal Research [Chapter 22 in *L.R.I.*; No Assignments] | --- |

24. Legal Citation Form [Chapter 23 in *L.R.I.*; No Assignments]    ---

25. Federal Tax Research [Not in *L.R.I.*; No Assignments]    ---

# Chapter 5

# FEDERAL COURT REPORTS

## ASSIGNMENT 1

## EXAMINATION OF UNITED STATES REPORTS

**Method:**

A.     Using the early volumes of *United States Reports* and the latest edition of *The Bluebook: A Uniform System of Citation*, find the *United States Reports* (U.S.) volume number for the following nominative reports. Put your answer in proper citation form.

**Questions:**

1.     8 Wheaton

2.     6 Cranch

3.     20 Wallace

4.     5 Peters

5.     24 Howard

6.     12 Wallace

7.     9 Cranch

8.     12 Wheaton

9.     8 Peters

10.     3 Dallas

11.     11 Wheaton

| | |
|---|---|
| 12. | 2 Black |
| 13. | 21 Howard |
| 14. | 13 Wallace |
| 15. | 8 Cranch |
| 16. | 4 Dallas |
| 17. | 1 Howard |
| 18. | 12 Peters |
| 19. | 7 Wallace |
| 20. | 20 Howard |

**Method:**

B.      Using the latest edition of *The Bluebook: A Uniform System of Citation* and *United States Reports* (U.S.), find the names of the following cases and cite them properly in your answer.

**Questions:**

| | |
|---|---|
| 1. | 340 U.S. 581 |
| 2. | 293 U.S. 388 |
| 3. | 283 U.S. 494 |
| 4. | 288 U.S. 290 |
| 5. | 300 U.S. 5 |
| 6. | 306 U.S. 451 |
| 7. | 315 U.S. 32 |
| 8. | 397 U.S. 337 |

9.      399 U.S. 66

10.     378 U.S. 368

11.     358 U.S. 133

12.     367 U.S. 643

13.     402 U.S. 415

14.     401 U.S. 154

15.     399 U.S. 66

16.     397 U.S. 254

17.     396 U.S. 435

18.     395 U.S. 752

19.     394 U.S. 576

20.     372 U.S. 335

21.     461 U.S. 190

22.     492 U.S. 257

23.     452 U.S. 594

24.     437 U.S. 385

25.     475 U.S. 673

26.     481 U.S. 279

## ASSIGNMENT 2

## UNITED STATES REPORTS - RELATED MATERIALS

**Method:**

For each of the citations to the official *United States Reports* (U.S.) locate the unofficial parallel citations in *West's Supreme Court Reporter* (S. Ct.) and *United States Supreme Court Reports, Lawyers' Edition* (L. Ed.).

**Questions:**

1. 358 U.S. 133

2. 402 U.S. 415

3. 399 U.S. 66

4. 394 U. S. 576

5. 372 U.S. 293

6. 340 U.S. 332

7. 293 U.S. 388

8. 288 U.S. 290

9. 300 U.S. 5

10. 306 U.S. 451

11. 315 U.S. 32

12. 378 U.S. 368

13. 376 U.S. 665

14. 380 U.S. 451

15. 386 U.S. 237

16.     390 U.S. 62

17.     395 U.S. 100

18.     405 U.S. 34

19.     406 U.S. 164

20.     411 U.S. 1

21.     437 U.S. 365

22.     462 U.S. 669

23.     475 U.S. 767

24.     485 U.S. 759

25.     492 U.S. 33

26.     469 U.S. 24

## ASSIGNMENT 3

## FEDERAL CASES

## Method:

A.    Using the set *Federal Cases* (F. Cas.) and the latest edition of *The Bluebook: A Uniform System of Citation*, find the names of the following cases and properly cite them.

## Questions:

    1.       Federal Case Number 358

    2.       Federal Case Number 18,210

    3.       Federal Case Number 7,881

    4.       Federal Case Number 9,317

    5.       Federal Case Number 2,865

    6.       Federal Case Number 1,424

    7.       Federal Case Number 2,344

    8.       Federal Case Number 3,555

    9.       Federal Case Number 6,994

    10.       Federal Case Number 13,753

    11.       Federal Case Number 9,596

    12.       Federal Case Number 11,825

    13.       Federal Case Number 8,260

    14.       Federal Case Number 14,249

    15.       Federal Case Number 15,959

**Method:**

B.     Using the Table of Citations in the Digest volume of *Federal Cases* (F.Cas.), locate the following cases.  Put your answer in proper citation form. [Instructions:  Locate the digest volume to the set *Federal Cases*.  Within it is a Table of Citations (these are on colored pages in the edition used by the editor)listing reporters alphabetically.  A parallel citation is given to the Federal Case Number.]

**Questions:**

1.      1 Fish. Pat. Cas. 483

2.      19 Int. Rev. Rec. 108

3.      5 Dill. 549

4.      1 Leg. Gaz. Rep. 279

5.      12 O.G. 1026

6.      1 McLean 120

7.      Abb. Adm. 529

8.      7 Biss. 426

9.      8 N.B.R. 525

10.     1 Lowell 91

11.     2 Sumn. 108

12.     2 McLean 464

13.     1 Bond 1

14.     4 Brewst. 250

15.     Spear, Extrad. (2d ed.) 451

**ASSIGNMENT 4**

**DRILL PROBLEMS AND THEME PROBLEMS**

**Drill Problem I:**

A.    Nominative Reports:

     1.       Using the early volumes of the *United States Reports*, give the official U.S. volume number citation for each of the following:
             (a)   1 Cranch
             (b)   7 Wheaton
             (c)   4 Dallas

     2.       Compare the volume designated 6 Cranch with 400 U.S. and answer the following questions:
             (a)   Contrast the features of the two volumes.
             (b)   Provide the full citation for the case that is printed in part on page 100 of each volume.

B.    *United States Reports* – Parallel Citations:

Using the parallel citations tables in the *West's Supreme Court Reporter* and the *United States Supreme Court Reports, Lawyers' Edition*, find the parallel citations for each of the following cases:

     1.       *Fuller v. Oregon*, 417 U.S. 40 (1974).

     2.       *Hanson v. Denckla*, 357 U.S. 235 (1958).

     3.       *Ring v. U.S.*, 419 U.S. 18 (1974).

     4.       *Piascik v. U.S.*, 434 U.S. 1062 (1978).

C.    *Lower Federal Court Cases:*

     1.       Using volume 425 of *Federal Reporter, Second Series*, answer the following:
             (a)   Who was the Circuit Justice for the Fifth Circuit?
             (b)   Give the correct cite for the case of *Boyk v. Mitchell*.
             (c)   Cite the case that defines "blatantly lawless."

2.      Using volume 300 of *Federal Supplement*, answer the following:
    (a)    Who is the Chief Judge of the U.S. Customs Court?
    (b)    Give the correct citation for *Bjarsch v. DiFalso*.
    (c)    What case defines the term "motorboat?"

3.      Using volume 200 of *Federal Reporter*, answer the following:
    (a)    What courts are covered by this volume?
    (b)    Who was the Chief Justice of the First Circuit Court of Appeals?
    (c)    On what page does the case of *Beradini v. Tocci* appear?
    (d)    What article and section of the Tennessee Constitution are construed in this volume?
    (e)    What is the docket number of *Arrow Transportation Co.*

4.      Using *Federal Cases*, answer the following:
    (a)    Give the full citation of the following cases:
        (1)    F. Cas. No. 5
        (2)    F. Cas. No. 25
    (b)    Give the Federal Case Number of the following cases:
        (1)    *Wood v. Wells*
        (2)    *Reid v. Rochereau*

## Drill Problem II:

A.   *Nominative Reports:*

1.      Give the full citation for the following cases. Using the latest edition of *The Bluebook,* put your answer in proper cite form.
    (a)    The case in volume 4 of the reports of John William Wallace at page 189.
    (b)    The case located in volume 16 of the reports of Richard Peters at page one.

2.      Making your answer complete and concise, compare volume 6 of Benjamin C. Howard's reports with volume 380 of the *United States Reports* in the following respects:
    (a)    Contrast the features of the two.
    (b)    Provide the full citation for the case appearing on page 163 of each volume.

B.  *United States Reports* – Parallel Citations:

Find the following cases in the *West's Supreme Court Reporter* and the United *States Supreme Court Reports, Lawyers' Edition* by using their parallel citation tables.  State volume and page.

1.  *Briscoe v. Bell*, 432 U.S. 404 (1977).

2.  *Zwicker v. Boll*, 391 U.S. 353 (1968).

3.  *Miami Herald Publishing Co. v. Tornillo*, 418 U.S. 241 (1974).

C.  *Lower Federal Court Cases:*

1.  Using volume 617 of the *Federal Reporter, Second Series*, answer the following:
    (a)  Who was the Chief Judge of the Second Circuit?
    (b)  Using the latest edition of *The Bluebook* give the correct citation for *Narenji v. Civiletti.*
    (c)  Cite the case defining "arbitrary."
    (d)  How many cases in this volume came from the Third Circuit?
    (e)  What case construed the American Bar Associaiton's Code of Professional Responsibility?  Properly cite it.

2.  Using volume 483 of *Federal Supplement*, answer the following:
    (a)  On what court did George H. Barlow sit prior to his death?
    (b)  Using the latest edition of *The Bluebook*, give the citation for the case defining "controversial."
    (c)  What case interpreted the Wisconsin Constitution?
    (d)  Who represented the plaintiff in *Hawkings-El v. Williams?*

3.  Using *Federal Cases*, answer the following:
    (a)  Give the full citation of Federal Case Number 3,914.
    (b)  Find the federal case number of *Ross v. Peaslee*.  Properly cite the case in your answer.

**Drill Problem III:**

A.  *Nominative Reports:*

1.  Give the full citation for the following cases.  Using the latest edition of *The Bluebook*, put your answer in proper cite form.

(a)   The case located in volume 20 of the reports of Benjamin C. Howard at page 486.

(b)   The case located in volume 2 of the reports of Henry Wheaton at page 248.

(c)   The case located in volume 4 of the reports of John William Wallace that deals with prisoners of war.

2.   Making your answer complete and concise, compare volume 16 of Richard Peters' reports with volume 418 of the *United States Reports* in the following respects:

(a)   Contrast the features of the two.

(b)   Provide the full citation for the case appearing on page 153 of each volume.

B.   *United States Reports* – Parallel Citations:

Find the following cases in the *West's Supreme Court Reporter* and the *United States Supreme Court Reports, Lawyers' Edition* by using their parallel citation tables.  State volume and page.

1.   *Blount v. Rizzi*, 400 U.S. 410 (1971).

2.   *Reading Co. v. Brown*, 391 U.S. 471 (1968).

3.   *Mandel v. Bradley*, 432 U.S. 173 (1977).

C.   *Lower Federal Court Cases:*

1.   Using volume 637 of the *Federal Reporter, Second Series* answer the following:

(a)   Each of the Justices of the Supreme Court serves as a Circuit Justice for one of the federal circuits.  As of the time of volume 637, who sat as the Circuit Justice for the Fourth Circuit?

(b)   Using the latest edition of *The Bluebook*, give the correct citation for the case interpreting Fed. R. Civ. Proc. 24(a).

(c)   Give the correct citation for the case defining "carry."

(d)   What states or political subdivisions are in the Third Circuit?

(e)   Who dissented in a case involving Roadway Express, Inc.?

2.   Using volume 497 of the *Federal Supplement*, answer the following:

(a) How many cases were decided by the District Court of Puerto Rico?

(b) Cite the case that defines "citizen."

(c) Cite the case interpreting the Alabama Code.

(d) What judge decided *United States v. Wenzel*?

3. Using *Federal Cases*, answer the following:

(a) Give the full citation of Federal Case Number 1,408.

(b) Find the Federal Case Number of *Clark v. Bininger*. Is there an opinion printed in *Federal Cases*?

**Theme Problem I:**

*Roe v. Wade* is one of the most talked about decisions of the past two decades. It can be found at 410 U.S. 113 (1973). Locate the case and answer the following questions:

1. Who wrote the majority opinion?

2. Is there a concurring opinion or opinions? If so, who wrote it, or them?

3. Is there a dissenting opinion or opinions? If so, who wrote it, or them?

4. What is the date of decision?

5. How many headnotes precede the case?

6. Who is Wade?

7. Who reargued the case for appellants?

8. *Roe v. Wade* can also be found at 93 S. Ct. 705 and 35 L. Ed. 2d 147. Look up each of these and answer the following:

(a) How many headnotes in each?

(b) What else is different about the opinions?

(c) Examine the "extras" in each volume: front matter, tables, and indexes, etc. List what's available in each.

(d) Are there any annotations in the *United States Supreme Court Reports, Lawyers' Edition*? If so, examine one.

9.       At 410 U.S. 155, the Court cites *Shapiro v. Thompson*, 394 U.S. 618 (1969). Locate that case.
         (a)    Answer questions 1-5 above for it.
         (b)    Locate the same (*Shapiro*) case in *West's Supreme Court Reporter* and *United States Supreme Court Reports, Lawyers' Edition, 2d.* Give the citations and answer questions 8(a) - 8(d) for this case.

10.      Also at 410 U.S. 155, the Court cites *Sherbert v. Verner*, 374 U.S. 398 (1963). Locate that case.
         (a)    Answer the questions 1-5 for it.
         (b)    Locate the same case in *West's Supreme Court Reporter* and *United States Supreme Court Reports, Lawyers' Edition, 2d.* Give the citations and answer the questions 8(a) - 8(d) for that case.

**Theme Problem II:**

*Gideon v. Wainwright* was a case of importance in setting out standards for criminal justice. It can be found at 372 U.S. 335 (1963). Locate the case and answer the following questions:

1.       What is the date of the decision?

2.       Who wrote the majority opinions?

3.       Is there a concurring opinion or opinions? Who wrote it, or them?

4.       Is there a dissenting opinion or opinions? Who wrote it, or them?

5.       Where did the case originate?

6.       Who argued the case for Gideon?

7.       Are there any headnotes?

8.       What is the result?

9.       *Gideon v. Wainwright* can also be found in the *West's Supreme Court Reporter* and *United States Supreme Court Reports, Lawyers' Edition, 2d.*

(a) Locate it, give the citations to the unofficial reporters.
(b) How many headnotes in each?
(c) Is there any difference in the opinions?
(d) Examine the "extras" available in each volume: front matter, tables and indexes, etc. List what is available in each.
(e) Are there any annotations in the *United States Supreme Court Reports, Lawyers' Edition*? If so, examine one.

10. At 372 U.S. 338 the Court cites *Betts v. Brady*. What is the official citation for *Betts*? Locate that case and answer questions 1-5 for that case.

11. At 372 U.S. 346, Justice Douglas cites *The Slaughter House Cases*, 16 Wall. 36. What other designation does 16 Wall. have? Locate that case and answer questions 1-5 for it.

12. What case does *Gideon v. Wainwright* overrule? Find the *West's Supreme Court Reporter* and *United States Supreme Court Reports Lawyers' Edition* citation for that case.

**Theme Problem III:**

Among the more controversial opinions you will likely encounter is that of Justice Cardozo in *Palsgraf v. Long Island R.R. Co.*, 248 N.Y. 339, 162 N.E. 99 (1928). There, in determining whether a woman on the platform of a train station could recover for injuries she received due to an explosion, Cardozo dealt at length with the topics of duty and foreseeability.

A. *Martinez v. California*, 444 U.S. 277 (1980) cites to *Palsgraf*. Answer the following with reference to *Martinez*.

1. Who wrote the opinion?

2. Who represented the Martinez family at oral argument?

3. Did any justice write a separate opinion?

4. What was the date of the decision?

5. Was *Palsgraf* necessary to the decision of the court?

B.    *Martinez* can also be found at 62 L.Ed.2d 481 and 100 S.Ct. 553.  Compare and contrast the treatment given the case in these reports and in the official version.

C.    *Palsgraf* is cited in 452 F.2d at 178.

    1.    Give the full citation for the case citing *Palsgraf.*

    2.    Which headnote(s) are supported by *Palsgraf?*

    3.    Who was the Chief Judge of the Seventh Circuit where the case was decided?

    4.    What states are served by the Seventh Circuit?

    5.    How many cases in 452 F.2d came to the Seventh Circuit from Wisconsin?

    6.    What case in 452 F.2d defines the term "transmission."  Properly cite it.

    7.    Who wrote the opinion in the case cited in question C-6?

    8.    What case in 452 F.2d cites to 21 U.S.C.A. § 355(h)?  Properly cite it.

**Theme Problem IV:**

*Sherwood v. Walker*, 66 Mich. 568, 33 N.W. 919 (1887) represents one of the fundamental cases dealing with mutual mistake in the making of contracts. In his dissenting opinion, Justice Sherwood of the Michigan Supreme Court attempts to distinguish *Allen v. Hammond*, 11 Pet. 63, on which the majority relies.

A.    Locate *Allen* and answer the following questions that relate to it.

    1.    What is its full citation?

    2.    Who wrote the majority opinion?

    3.    Did any justices write separate opinions?

    4.    Who was the Chief Justice at the time of the decision?

    5.    Who argued for the appellee?

B.    The same case can be found at 9 L. Ed. 633.

    1.    Compare and contrast the two reports.

    2.    Why does the case not appear in *West's Supreme Court Reporter*?

C.    *Sherwood* is discussed in 621 F.2d at 1349.

    1.    Give the full citation of the case that cites *Sherwood.*

    2.    For which headnote is *Sherwood* cited?

    3.    Who wrote the opinion?

    4.    Who dissented?

    5.    Who was Chief Judge of the Fifth Circuit at the time?

    6.    At the time, what states were located in the Fifth Circuit?

    7.    How many cases arose in West Virginia that were reported in 621 F.2d?

    8.    What case in 621 F.2d cites the Rules of the Supreme Court of the United States?

# Chapter 6

# STATE COURT REPORTS AND
# THE NATIONAL REPORTER SYSTEM

## ASSIGNMENT 1

## COURT REPORTS

**Questions:**

1. The opinions of what courts in your state are published in any form--official or unofficial?

2. List the current official and unofficial reports for your state.

3. In what form do the official decisions in your state first appear, i.e., slip opinion, advance sheet, bound volume?

4. Compare a current volume of the *California Reporter* and a current volume of the *Pacific Reporter*. The opinions of which California court are duplicated?

5. Compare a current volume of the *New York Supplement* and a current volume of the *North Eastern Reporter*. The opinions of what New York court are duplicated in both reporters?

6. Examine a current volume of the *National Reporter System* regional unit that includes your state. Find the "Table of Contents" and list the material contained in this volume.

7. Examine volume 484 P.2d. Cite the pages of the two table of cases which cite *Riddell v. Rhay.*

8. Give the complete citation to a case in 189 N.W.2d that construes the following statute: North Dakota Century Code 1-02-10.

9. Give the citation to a case and the page number of the case in 183 S.E.2d that defines the word "war."

10. Examine the Key Number digest section of volume 470 S.W.2d. Give the subject, key number, and citation to the first case digested.

11. Examine the case in volume 273 N.E.2d at page 252. Answer the following:
    (a) What is the name of the case?
    (b) What is the docket number?
    (c) What is the name of the court?

12. Examine the case of E. & E. Newman, Inc. v. Hallock at 281 A.2d 544. Answer the following:
    (a) What is the official state report citation for this case, if any?
    (b) How many different key numbers are listed in the headnotes of this case?

13. Examine the case of *De Palma v. State*, 185 S.E.2d 53. Answer the following:
    (a) Headnotes 3, 4, and 5 are discussed on which page of the opinion?
    (b) Syllabus 4(b) of the court is discussed on which page of the opinion?

14. Cases in the National Reporter System units appear first in advance sheet form.
    (a) Is the pagination in the advance sheets the same as that in the bound volume?
    (b) Will the text of the cases found in the advance sheets always be the same as that in the bound volumes which replace them?

15. The Key Number Digest section is located at the end of each bound volume of the National Reporter system. Where is the Key Number Digest section located in the National Reporter System advance sheets?

16. Examine volume 113 A.2d. Cite the pages of the two tables of cases which cite *Bata v. Hill.*

17. Give the complete citation to a case in volume 97 N.E.2d which construes Article 8, sec. 4 of the Ohio Constitution.

18. Give the citation to a case in 106 Cal. Rptr. that defines the word "revolver," and the page number on which the definition is found.

19. Examine the Key Number digest section of volume 201 N.Y.S.2d. Give the subject, Key Number, and citation to the first case digested.

20. Examine the case in volume 89 So.2d at page 459. Answer the following:
    - (a) What is the name of the case?
    - (b) What is the docket number?
    - (c) What is the name of the court?

21. Examine the case of *State v. Waid* at 67 P.2d 647. Answer the following:
    - (a) Is the official state report citation given for this case?
    - (b) How many different Key Numbers are listed in the headnotes of this case?

22. Examine the case of *United States Cold Storage Corp. v. Stolinski*, 96 N.W.2d 408. Answer the following:
    - (a) Headnotes 8, 9 are discussed on what page?
    - (b) Syllabus 2 of the court is found on what page?

23. Examine the case of *Green v. State*, 209 S.W.2d 195. Answer the following:
    - (a) In what court was the appeal heard?
    - (b) What were the names of the attorneys for the appellant?
    - (c) What was the name of the judge who wrote the opinion of the court?
    - (d) What was the name of the judge who wrote the opinion on the appellant's motion for rehearing?

# ASSIGNMENT 2

## PARALLEL CITATIONS

**Method:**

Using the *National Reporter System Blue Books* and Supplements, provide the parallel citation for each citation given below.

**Questions:**

1.  245 Ala. 411

2.  20 Cal. App. 252

3.  110 Ind. 294

4.  97 S.C. 261

5.  86 Tex. Cr. 620

6.  340 Mass. 334

7.  75 N.J. Super. 192

8.  198 Pa. Super. 169

9.  69 Wash. 2d 144

10.  83 Nev. 1

11.  173 Ga. App. 37

12.  221 Neb. Rep. 409

13.  41 Ohio App. Rep. 3rd 138

14.  474 Penn. St. Rep. 570

15.  255 S.C. Rep. 570

16.  33 Mich. App. Rep. 294

# ASSIGNMENT 3

## USE OF TABLE OF CASES

**Method:**

Using the table of cases in the reporter volumes shown, provide the proper pagination.

**Questions:**

1.     *Adler v. Bush Terminal Co.*, 291 N.Y.S.

2.     *Hensel v. Cahill*, 116 A.2d

3.     *State ex rel. Harbage v. Ferguson*, 36 N.E.2d

4.     *Burt  v. Munger*, 23 N.W.2d

5.     *Handley v. Jackson*, 51 P.

6.     *Strickland v. Johnson*, 197 S.E.

7.     *Savage v. Olson*, 9 So.2d

8.     *Owens v. Daniel*, 16 S.W.2d

9.     *Bodrey v. Bodrey*, 161 S.E.2d

10.     *Weddle v. Cox*, 394 P.2d

# ASSIGNMENT 4

## USE OF VOLUME DIGEST

## Method:

Using the digest to the reporter volumes shown, provide the citation to the appropriate cases.

## Questions:

1.  A case in 110 A.2d concerning the liability of warehousemen to the owners of goods which are lost, destroyed, or damaged.

2.  A case in 71 Cal. Rptr. concerning certainty and definiteness as requisites of a statute.

3.  A case in 218 N.Y.S.2d concerning the effect of old age on the testamentary capacity to make a will.

4.  A case in 18 N.E.2d concerning acts or conduct constituting contempt of court.

5.  A case in 538 S.W.2d concerning limiting the time or scope of argument of counsel.

6.  A case in 223 So.2d concerning the care required and liability in general of inn keepers.

7.  A case in 472 P.2d concerning the nature and theory of the right of subrogation.

8.  A case in 308 A.2d concerning injury to or destruction of fish.

9.  A case in 154 N.W.2d concerning discretion of the court relating to new trial.

10. A case in 59 N.E.2d concerning nature of a constructive trust.

# ASSIGNMENT 5

## USE OF THE TABLE OF STATUTES CONSTRUED

**Method:**

Using the table of statutes construed for the reporter volumes shown, provide the citation to the appropriate case.

**Questions:**

1. Uniform Fraudulent Conveyance Act. §4 (112 A .2d).

2. 26 U.S.C.A. §1033 (72 Cal. Rptr.).

3. U.S. CONST., amend. I (203 N.Y.S.2d).

4. Ohio General Codes, § 26 (65 N.E.2d).

5. Uniform Commercial Code, § 2-201 (2) (536 S.W.2d).

6. Louisiana Code of Criminal Procedure, art. 920 (308 So.2d).

7. U.S. CONST. art. IV, 1 (535 P.2d).

8. South Dakota Compiled Laws, 1-26-36 (195 N.W.2d).

9. N.Y. TOWN LAW 268 (2) (229 N.Y.S.2d).

10. PA. RULES CRIM. P. 150 (340 A.2d).

# ASSIGNMENT 6

## USE OF WORDS AND PHRASES

**Method:**

Using the Words and Phrases section of the reporter volumes shown, provide the citation to the appropriate case.

**Questions:**

1.    "Employer," 85 Cal. Rptr.

2.    "Direct Evidence," 83 N.E.2d.

3.    "Enclosed Structure," 534 S.W.2d.

4.    "Child," 108 P.2d.

5.    "Mutual," 152 N.W.2d.

6.    "Duress," 49 N.E.2d.

7.    "Unfitness," 128 N.W.2d.

8.    "Domicile," 85 N.E.2d.

9.    "Reasonable," 204 N.W.2d.

10.   "Lapsed Legacy," 173 N.Y.S.2d.

# ASSIGNMENT 7

## THEME PROBLEMS AND DRILL PROBLEMS

**Theme Problem I:**

A.     *Brown v. Board of Education* is cited at 358 A.2d 835. Locate this decision and answer the following questions about the case that contains it.

      1.     What is the name and citation of the case that cites *Brown*?

      2.     What is the official citation?

      3.     Who represented defendant Evans?

      4.     If you wanted to find other cases in this volume dealing with the same point for which *Brown* is cited, how would you do it?

      5.     What states does this reporter cover?

      6.     Give the name and citation of any case in this volume that mentions the Constitution of New Hampshire.

      7.     Give the name and citation of a case in this volume that defines "startling event."

      8.     Who was the chief justice of the Maine Supreme Judicial Court when *Rybeck* was rendered?

B.     *Brown v. Board of Education* is also cited at 223 S.E.2d 617 in a dissent. Locate this citation and answer the following questions concerning the case in which the citation is found:

      1.     What is the name and citation of the case?

      2.     Is there an official citation given?  If so, what is it?

      3.     Who wrote the dissent that cited *Brown*?

      4.     Why does no headnote cover the part of the opinion in which the citation of *Brown* occurs?

      5.     What other states are covered by this reporter?

6.    Give the name and citation of any case in this volume that cites the North Carolina Code of Judicial Conduct.

7.    Who was the chief judge of the Georgia Court of Appeals at the time this case was decided?

A.    *Roe v. Wade* cites the case found at 354 S.W.2d 161.  Locate this case and answer the following questions concerning it.

1.    Give the correct name and citation of the case.

2.    Note there is no official citation. List two reasons why this may be.

3.    Who represented the state?

4.    What is the result?

5.    If you wanted to find other cases in this volume on the topic covered under headnote seven, how could you do it?

6.    Give the names and citations of any cases in this volume that interpret the Kentucky Constitution.

7.    Who was the presiding judge of the Kansas City (Missouri) Court of Appeals when this case was decided?

B.    *Roe v. Wade* also cites to 250 So.2d 857.  Locate that case and answer the following questions concerning it.

1.    Give the correct name and citation of this case.

2.    List the counsel who participated.

3.    List any concurring opinions.

4.    What is the result?

5.    If one wanted to locate other cases in this volume that deal with the point covered in headnote 1, how could one do it?

6.    What other states are covered by this reporter?

7.    Give the names and citations of any cases in this volume that mention the Florida Code of Ethics.

8.    Where in this volume could one find the opinion in *Rachal v. Rachal?*

9.    Name the person who was presiding judge of the Louisiana 3rd Circuit Court of Appeals as of the decision in *Walsingham.*

**Theme Problem III:**

A.    Answer the following with regard to *Palsgraf*, 162 N.E. 99

1.    What is the citation in the official reporter?

2.    Give the full names of the three dissenting judges.

3.    Who represented the railroad?

4.    What other jurisdictions are reported in this volume?

B.    *Palsgraf* is referred to at 350 N.Y.S.2d 651. Answer the following with regard to that case:

1.    Give its full citation, indicating on what page the court cites to *Palsgraf.*

2.    For what reason does it refer to Cardozo?

3.    Cite another case in the volume which defines "motorcycle."

4.    What case in the volume deals with the first amendment to the United States Constitution?

**Theme Problem IV:**

A.    *Sherwood v. Walker* can be found at 33 N.W. 919. Look at the case and answer the following questions:

1.    What is the citation in the official reporter?

2.    What other jurisdictions are represented in the same volume?

B.    *Sherwood* is referred to at 294 N.W. 708. Answer the following questions relating to that case:

    1.    What is the full citation?

    2.    How does the organization of its headnotes differ from *Sherwood*?

    3.    What is the full name of the justice who wrote the opinion?

C.    A later Michigan case extends the concept of mistake from a settlement agreement to vacating a consent judgment at 185 N.W.2d 64.

    1.    Who represented the City of Warren in that case?

    2.    What case in the same volume defines "abuse of discretion?"

    3.    How may cases in the volume come from South Dakota?

**Drill Problem I:**

Use the *National Reporter System*. Answer as concisely as possible.

    1.    *Parallel Citations.* Give the *National Reporter* citation for the following cases. Use the *National Reporter Blue Books*.
        (a) 363 Mo. 442.
        (b) 264 Ind. 313.
        (c) 280 MD.332.

    2.    Features of the *National Reporter System* volumes.
        (a)    *Table of Cases.* Using the volume shown, provide the page citation for the listed cases.
        (i) In 477 S.W.2d, *Travelers Ins. Co. v. Speer.*
        (ii) In 520 P.2d, *State v. Clark*
        (iii) In 290 N.E.2d, *Slocum v. Fire and Police Comm. of City of East Peoria.*

        (b)    *Statutes Construed.* Using the volume shown, provide the page citation to the case that cites the following statute.
        (i)    In 344 A.2d, Rule 803(6) of the U.S. Federal Rules of Evidence.

    (ii)  In 568 S.W.2d, Art 6, §9 of the Tennessee
       Constitution.

## Drill Problem II:

Use the *National Reporter System.* Answer as concisely as possible.

  1.  Parallel Citations. Give the *National Reporter* citation for the
    following cases. Use the *National Reporter Blue Books.*
      (a)  76 Cal. App. 3d 302.
      (b)  240 Ga. 479.
      (c)  85 Idaho 226.

  2.  Features of the *National Reporter System* volumes.
    (a)  *Table of Cases.* Using the volume shown, provide the
      page citation for the listed cases.
      (i)  In 167 S.E.2d, *Young v. State.*
      (ii)  In 232 N.E. 2d, *Zoppo Co. v. Com.*
      (iii)  In 539 P.2d, *Zylstra v. Piva.*

    (b)  *Statutes Construed.* Using the volume shown, provide the
      page citation of the case that cites the following statute.
      (i)  In 583 P.2d, Kansas Statues Annot. 21-
        3302.

## Drill Problem III:

A.  Parallel Citations.

  1.  187 Kan. 458.

  2.  10 N.Y.2d 859.

  3.  4 N.C. App. 652.

B.  Using the volume indicated, provide the full citation for the following
cases:

  1.  In 364 So.2d, a case in which the Shell Oil Company was the
    defendant.

  2.  In 213 S.E.2d, a case in which George Vick was the defendant.

  3.  In 564 S.W.2d, a case construing the Texas Election Code.

4.    In 237 N.W.2d, a case defining "Criminal Assault."

5.    In 399 N.E.2d, a case dealing with Fines.

6.    In 582 P.2d, a case from Utah involving a sugar company.


**Drill Problem IV:**

A.    *Parallel Citations.*

1.    141 Ga. App. 678.

2.    265 Ind. 616.

3.    115 R.I. 303.

B.    Using the volume indicated, provide the full citation for the following cases:

1.    A case in 424 A.2d, in which Barry Brann sued the State of Maine.

2    A case in 415 N.E.2d, in which John Green was the defendant.

3    A case in 283 N.W.2d, construing Mich. Comp. Laws §430.53.

4.    A case in 614 P.2d, defining "Arms."

5.    A case in 273 S.E.2d, dealing with products liability.

6.    A case in 621 P.2d, dealing with a taxicab company, decided by the Nevada Supreme Court.

# Chapter 7

# DIGESTS FOR COURT REPORTS

## ASSIGNMENT 1

## USE OF THE AMERICAN DIGEST SYSTEM

**Method:**

Using the indexes of the *Decennial Digest* specified at the beginning of each problem, carry out the following six steps in accord with the example given in the beginning of the problems:

(1)     Answer the question with a "yes" or "no," basing your answer on information found in the specified digest.

(2)     List the Topic and Key Numbers(s) under which the digest paragraph was found.

(3)     Using the Topic Outline, what is the specific subject of the Topic and Key Number(s)?

(4)     Using the latest edition of *The Bluebook* for proper form, give the case name and full citation to which the digest paragraph you located applies.

(5)     Are there any cases in the first ten volumes of the *General Digest Twelfth Series* under the same Topic and Key Number(s) as found in (2) *supra*? Answer with either the specific volume number(s) or the word "none."

(6)     Give the corresponding or most nearly similar Century Digest (1658-1896) Topic and Section Number for the Topic and Key Number in (2) *supra*.

**Example:**

QUESTION:     Use *Fifth Decennial*. Mr. Ned Lee of Webster County, Mississippi, sued the Memphis, Tennessee Publishing Company, a Delaware Corporation, for damages arising out of an allegedly defamatory and libelous article published by the defendant. Service of process was effected against, among others, the Secretary of State of the State of Mississippi. Defendant moved for dismissal based on lack of jurisdiction, stating it was not "present" within the state, that it was not doing business within the State of Mississippi, and that (by implication) it would violate due process of law contrary to Section I of Article XIV of the U.S. Constitution to subject defendant to local jurisdiction. Should the defendant prevail?

ANSWER:
(1) Yes.
(2) Constitutional Law 309(3).
(3) Constitutional Law - Due Process of Law - Civil Remedies and Proceedings – Parties and Process or Notice – Service on Agent of Nonresident.
(4) *Lee v. Memphis Pub. Co.*, 195 Miss. 264, 14 So. 2d 351 (1943).
(5) None.
(6) Constitutional Law -- §§ 929-30.

## Questions:

1.    Use *First Decennial*. In a civil case, the postmark on a letter was introduced into evidence. Is the postmark admissible into evidence without proof?

2.    Use *Second Decennial*. Eddie Norton was adjudged an incompetent by of reason habitual drunkenness. Are Eddie's subsequent contracts which affect his property rendered void by this adjudication?

3.    Use *Third Decennial*. A petition was filed with the Minnesota Board of Law Examiners seeking the disbarment of an attorney for alleged misconduct in signing a will as a witness after the testatrix had died. Was the evidence of this alleged misconduct sufficient to sustain the charge?

4.    Use *Fourth Decennial*. Plaintiff sued for rent under a written lease. After finding for the defendant, plaintiff contended that the court lacked jurisdiction since the order had been entered before return to proof of service had been filed. In New Hampshire does failure to file the return deny the court jurisdiction?

5.    Use *Fifth Decennial*. Relying on the Mississippi statute which provided that one was presumed dead if absent for seven years without having been heard from, Freda, whose first husband had

been absent and not heard from for more than seven years, married Bill. Subsequent to Freda's marriage to Bill it was discovered that Freda's first husband was alive. Was the marriage of Freda and Bill void?

6. Use *Sixth Decennial.* Mr. Lawrence Hawthorne borrowed two sums ($45,000 and $18,000) in 1954 from his partners, Mr. and Mrs. J. M. Walton, and was charged an illegally high interest rate. Mr. Hawthorne repaid the sums and interest, and then sued to recover the excess interest. Has Mr. Hawthorne waived or released his claim of usury by payment?

7. Use *Sixth Decennial.* Mr. Kinzer was indicted for housebreaking and larceny. The trial ended with a hung jury. During the second trial, Kinzer's counsel moved to subpoena the court reporter from the first trial, for use in cross-examination of government witnesses, after the court denied defendant's request for a free transcript. Disregarding the trial court's denials of defendant's motions, as a general rule will stenographers or reporters notes, taken at a former trial, be dismissed to impeach testimony of witnesses?

8. Use *Seventh Decennial.* An actress entered into a contract with an agency to be her exclusive representative for a period of five years. Under the contract she was to pay the agency 10% of her earnings. Simultaneously the agency allegedly made an oral agreement to pay 5% of her earnings to another agent to whom she was already under contract. In New York, does the statute of frauds bar enforcement of such an oral agreement made in conjunction with an artist's exclusive agency contract?

9. Use *Seventh Decennial.* Twice daily a farmer drove his herd of cattle along the main road through a village in Maryland from his barn on one edge of the village to his pasture on the opposite edge. Residents of the village complained that the dropping of manure on the roadway was a nuisance and sought to enjoin the farmer from driving his cattle through the village. In Maryland, does the driving of cattle along a public highway to pasture constitute a nuisance per se?

10. Use *Seventh Decennial.* Walter J. Borowicz, five years old, was injured in Maplewood, New Jersey, when he was struck by William J. Hood's car. Walter's parents sued Mr. Hood. A

policeman, Officer Schuler, testified that he had measured Mr. Hood's skid marks as 63 feet in length. As instructions regarding speed and control of the automobile where injuries resulted from the negligent operation of the vehicle, should the court have instructed the jury as to the skidding?

11.     Use *Seventh Decennial.* Mrs. Geneva Rose and Lawrence Rose, the widow and son, respectively, of the decedent, were sentenced to 10 years for slaying John Rose. Only circumstantial evidence was introduced and that evidence was conflicting. Was this sufficient proof of guilt as to a homicide under criminal law?

12.     Use *Seventh Decennial.* Mr. Gary Mullendore was rear-ended while he was stopped in a line of Kansas City traffic. He sued and won. The defendant appealed, claiming the trial court erred in giving an instruction allowing the jury to assess damages for mental suffering even though there had been no testimony to that effect. Was defendant's appeal successful?

13.     Use *Seventh Decennial.* At the close of a rather lengthy trial, a jury determined that the decedent's gift three years prior to death had been a valid inter vivos gift, and judgment was rendered in favor of the defendant recipient of the gift. Plaintiff appealed, challenging the jury's finding of fact with respect to intent, delivery, and acceptance. Was the jury's determination allowed to stand on appeal?

14.     Use *Eighth Decennial.* Mr. Louis discovered some heretofore unpublished letters and intended to include those letters in a book. These letters were written by a husband and wife to their children. The children's parents were convicted of treason and ultimately executed. The children attempt to enjoin publication of these letters claiming they are copyrighted. Does the "fair use" doctrine permit use of these materials if it is done in a reasonable manner?

15.     Use *Eighth Decennial.* Sandra and Harry Henry were on a trip across Massachusetts when their car was struck by defendant's vehicle. Sandra was pregnant with viable twin fetuses which were subsequently stillborn. Sandra filed a wrongful death action on behalf of the estates of the two children. Is a stillborn child, a "person" under the Massachusetts Wrongful Death statute?

16. Use *Eighth Decennial.* A prison inmate was burned over thirty percent of his body when another inmate hurled a "Molotov Cocktail" into his cell. As a result, the inmate was hospitalized for four months, underwent painful skin grafts, and suffered severe nightmares. He was awarded $25,000 for past and future suffering. Were these damages excessive?

17. Use *Eighth Decennial.* Mary responded to a beauty parlor advertisement for a permanent and wave for only $12.50. The beautician suggested a more expensive and different treatment. Mary agreed. Within a few days her hair became dry and brittle and broke whenever she brushed it. To hide her embarrassment she bought several hair pieces and later took hair treatments to stop her hair from breaking off at the scalp. A jury awarded damages of over $2,000 for her suffering and out of pocket expenses. Was this award reasonable?

18. Use *Eighth Decennial.* A New York pharmacist advertised through local newspapers discounts on all drug needs and offered free $2.00 certificates for use with all drug purchases. The State Board of Pharmacy charged that this advertising practice was unethical and a violation of a state regulation prohibiting the advertising of discount prescriptions. Was this regulation found to be unconstitutionally vague?

# ASSIGNMENT 2

## USE OF TABLES TO CONVERT FROM CENTURY DIGEST SECTION NUMBERS TO DECENNIAL DIGEST KEY NUMBERS

**Method:**

Refer either to Volume 21 of the *First Decennial Digest* or to Volume 24 of the *Second Decennial Digest*. Using the table in either location (they're identical), convert the below-listed *Century Digest* Section Numbers to appropriate *Decennial Digest* Key Numbers.

**Example:**

QUESTION:     Licenses § 41
ANSWER:        Animals - 4

**Questions:**

1.     Attorney and Client § 199

2.     Bankruptcy § 735

3.     Burglary § 35

4.     Contracts § 517

5.     Criminal Law §1247

6.     Discovery § 55

7.     Eminent Domain § 223

8.     Fish § 12

9.     Guaranty § 38

10.    Homicide § 549

11.    Infants § 177

12.    Landlord and Tenant § 567

13.     Mortgages § 1608

14.     Navigable Waters § 107

15.     Obscenity § 16

16.     Parent and Child § 76

17.     Statutes § 56

18.     Taxation § 104

19.     Usury § 219

20.     Wills § 1630

## ASSIGNMENT 3

## USE OF U.S. SUPREME COURT DIGESTS

**Method:**

Using either Lawyers Cooperative Publishing's *U.S. Supreme Court Reports Digest, (Lawyers' Edition)* or West's *U.S. Supreme Court Digest,* answer the problems listed below and provide:

(1)  A "Yes" or "No" answer to the question, basing your reply on a relevant digest paragraph.

(2)  The "Lawyers' Edition Digest" Topic and Section Number or the "West's U.S. Digest" Topic and Key Number which covers the digest paragraph which answers the question.

(3)  The complete citation to the case in point using the latest edition of *A Uniform System of Citation* for proper form.

**Example:**

QUESTION:  Has the United States Supreme Court spoken about the justification for punishing libels according to Illinois law? (1952)

ANSWER:  (1)  Yes.

(2)  (a)  Lawyers' Edition Digest: Libel and Slander

(b)  West's U.S. Digest: Libel & Slander - 141

(c)  *Beauharnais v. Illinois,* 343 U.S. 250 (1952).

**Questions:**

1.  Does the existence of a statutory right imply the existence of all necessary and appropriate remedies? (1969)

2.  Does a father have a constitutionally protected right to the custody, care, and management of his children? (1975)

3.  Can a person other than a citizen take an oath to support the Constitution of the United States? (1973)

4.  Does the accidental destruction of a house by fire relieve the lessee of liability for rent? (1868)

5.  An oral confession was used which was made to a doctor at a hospital one hour after the arrest of the defendant who had been shot and had been given two large injections of morphine. Is this in violation of due process? (1972)

6.  Is evidence by comparison of handwritings admissible when the witness had had no previous knowledge of the writings, but is called on to testify merely from a comparison? (1870)

7.  A contract was signed by one of the parties on Sunday, and delivered to an agent of the other party. The assent and signature of the other party were not given until a weekday. Was the contract void, being in violation of a statute making it penal to do any manner of business on Sunday? (1884)

8.  A testator gave certain real and personal property to a city in trust, forever, for the purpose of building and supporting two colleges. None of the property purchased therefore was to be sold, ever. Is this void as creating a perpetuity? (1860)

9.  May a witness in federal criminal prosecution be asked leading questions if the inference which will be drawn from the question is factually true? (1961)

10. May a state arbitrarily deny admission to practice law? (1961)

11. Would a zoning ordinance which is clearly arbitrary and unreasonable and without substantial relation to public health, safety, or general welfare be declared unconstitutional? (1926)

12. Is a particular form of words essential to create a trust, provided there is reasonable certainty as to the property, the objects, and the beneficiaries? (1920)

13. A statute of state A required all marriages to be entered into in the presence of a magistrate or clergyman and required that the marriage be preceded by a license. The statute was silent as to whether a marriage not complying with its provisions was void. X and Y did not follow this formal procedure but lived together

as husband and wife. They claim a common law marriage and that, therefore, their marriage is valid. Are they correct? (1877)

14. Does the fact that an alien plaintiff resides in the same state as defendant deprive the federal courts from having jurisdiction over the case? (1853)

15. The legislature of state A passed a special act granting X a divorce from Y. Is this divorce valid even though not given by a court of competent jurisdiction? (1888)

16. If an attorney had been appointed *by* the court to represent an accused, must the attorney do so? (1932)

17. The public health law of state X provides that any doctor practicing medicine after being convicted of a felony shall be guilty of a misdemeanor. Is this provision valid? (1898)

18. X had for many years occupied certain public lands of the U.S. Government. Subsequently, the federal government granted a plot of land to Y. This plot included that land occupied by X. X claims to have obtained the government's land by adverse possession and that the grant of the land by the government to Y is therefore void. Is this contention correct? (1877)

19. A took from B a mortgage on certain real estate containing sandstone quarries which, however, had not been sufficiently worked to determine their extent or value. B, C, and D certified that they had resided in the neighborhood for 20 years and that in their best opinion and judgment the value of the quarry was 150 per cent more than the loan. Upon foreclosure the land brought less than one-sixth the amount of the loan. A sued B, C, and D for damages caused him by their fraud and misrepresentation. Can A recover? (1881)

20. The Georgia House of Representatives refused to seat a duly elected representative because of his statements attacking the policy of the Federal Government in Vietnam and the Selective Service laws. Was this refusal unconstitutional based on denial of freedom of speech? (1966)

21. Is involuntary commitment more than a loss of freedom from confinement? (1980)

# ASSIGNMENT 4

## USE OF THE MODERN FEDERAL PRACTICE DIGEST, WEST'S FEDERAL PRACTICE DIGEST, 2d, WEST'S FEDERAL PRACTICE DIGEST, 3d, AND WEST'S FEDERAL PRACTICE DIGEST, 4th

**Method:**

Refer to the *Modern Federal Practice Digest, West's Federal Practice Digest, 2d West's Federal Practice Digest, 3d,* or to *West's Federal Practice Digest, 4th.* The date the case was decided is given in parenthesis at the end of each problem. In relation to each problem, provide:

(1) A "Yes" or "No" answer to the question contained in the problem.
(2) The Topic and Key Number under which you found the digest paragraph that answered (1), *supra.*
(3) The complete citation to the case in point using the latest edition of *The Bluebook* for proper form.

**Example:**

QUESTION:    Presume that a federal taxpayer has no office, no telephone, no furniture, no seal, and does not hold any meetings. Do these facts establish that the taxpayer is not an association taxable as a corporation? (1942)

ANSWER:    (1)    No
(2)    Internal Revenue - 815
(3)    *Keating-Snyder Trust v. Commissioner,* 126 F.2d 860 (5th Cir. 1942).

**Questions:**

1. According to the Nebraska federal trial court, may a public officer charge the person benefited by a service, for additional compensation, absent express statutory authorization? (1946)

2.      May the doctrine of *res ipsa loquitur* be applied under Idaho law in a malpractice action against a physician? (1973)

3.      Has any federal court ever passed on the effect to First Amendment rights of free speech concerning the White House restrictions on demonstrations which put a damper on the use of streets and public places for demonstration purposes? (1973)

4.      According to the Second Circuit's interpretation of 18 U.S.C. § 922(a)(3), is scienter an element of the statute making it unlawful to transport into one's state of residence a firearm or other weapons purchased outside the state? (1973)

5.      Does a bank have the right to countermand a traveler's check which it has issued? (1942)

6.      Does a purchaser of a cemetery lot acquire a property right which the law recognizes? (1950)

7.      Is a lawyer an "officer of the court" within the meaning of the statute empowering courts to punish as contempt misbehavior of its officers in their official transactions? (1956)

8.      Under Tennessee law, is a hospital strictly liable for administering a transfusion of blood which is infected with serum hepatitis? (1975)

9.      Does the use of force to obtain a legitimate union demand for higher wages evidence the requisite intent for conviction of extortion? (1973)

10.     A village passed an ordinance prohibiting the flight of aircraft over the village at an altitude of less than 1,000 feet. Is the ordinance constitutional? (1952)

11.     Is proof of conversion to the defendant's use essential to every conviction for embezzlement of CETA funds? (1984)

12.     Is a contract of some nature, either express or implied in fact, essential to the right of an attorney to recover for expenses? (1980)

13.     May the government break down a single conspiracy into component sub-agreements for purpose of multiple punishments or multiple prosecution? (1977)

14.     Does fact that relevant means of knowledge was readily available and open to plaintiff but remained unused preclude liability for willful fraud? (1980)

15.     Generally, is there privity between an injured party and the insurer of a wrongdoer? (1984)

16.     Is disclosure of a competency report mandated even where the report indicates insanity or incompetency? (1978)

17.     Can an ordinance of a municipal corporation which is not over broad be nevertheless unconstitutional as applied if it is enforced against a protected activity? (1976)

18.     Is use of corporal punishment to discipline public school students forbidden simply because it interferes in some instances with the right of parental control? (1976)

19.     Does the use of the word "radio" in the Communications Act include television transmission? (1984)

20.     Does a statute which makes punishable, inter alia, the receipt of a firearm by an ex-felon infringe on the right to bear arms? (1976).

21.     Does placing developmentally disabled persons in state-sponsored institutions, rather than in community facilities violate equal protection? (1990)

22.     Does the act of producing documents have testimonial aspects to which the privilege against self-incrimination may apply? (1988)

23.     Do charges of immorality, dishonesty, etc., in the dismissal of a government employee infringe a liberty interest when an individual's reputation and good name are at stake? (1990)

# ASSIGNMENT 5

## USE OF THE TABLES OF CASES
## OF THE AMERICAN DIGEST SYSTEM

**Method:**

Check the Table of Cases of the appropriate portion of the American Digest System. Locate the following and provide:

(1)   The West reporter citation.  Do not provide parallel, memo, cert. or rehearing citations.

(2)   The first-listed Topic and its first Key Number.

**Example:**

QUESTION:        *Heinbach v. Heinbach* (1918)
ANSWER:          (1)    202 S.W. 1123
                 (2)    Acknowledgment - 54

**Questions:**

1.   *Robards v. Rees* (1986)

2.   *Adoptive Parents v. Superior Court in and for Maricopa County* (1970)

3.   *Boies v. Dovico* (1965)

4.   *Cain v. Meade County* (1929)

5.   *State v. Feeler* (1982)

6.   *Daugherty v. Feland* (1916)

7.   *Dorsey v. Petrott* (1940)

8.   *Eustace v. Speckhart* (1973)

9.   *U-Hail Co. v. Liberty Mut. Ins. Co.* (1984)

10.     *Faulk v. Soberanes* (1961)

11.     *Holman v. Oriental Refinery* (1965)

12.     *Ivanhoe Grand Lodge AF & AM of Colo. v. Most Worshipful Grand Lodge of Ancient Free and Accepted Masons of Colo.* (1952)

13.     *Leathers v. Tupelo Coffee Co.* (1982)

14.     *Julian v. Harris* (1973)

15.     *King v. Flemming* (1961)

16.     *Levin v. Sohn* (1948)

17.     *Milburn v. McNiff* (1985)

18.     *Perkins v. C.I.R.* (1984)

19.     *Mile High Poultry Farms v. Frazier* (1945)

20.     *Quinlan v. Bussiere* (1965)

21.      *Oregon v. Niles* (1985)

22.     *Southern Seating & Cabinet Co. v. Gladish* (1916)

23.     *BA Leasing Corp. v. Board of Assessment Appeals of State of Colo.* (1982)

24.     *State ex rel Quigg v. Liquidator of Sewer Districts of St. Louis County* (1943)

25.     *Tener v. Hill* (1965)

26.     *Dedek v. Dedek* (1984)

27.     *United States v. Varlack* (1955)

28.     *Velez v. Christian* (1973)

29.     *Flynn, In re Paternity of* (1983)

30.    *Citron v. E.I. DuPont de Nemour & Co.* (1990)

32.    *Byrd v. Aetna Cas. & Sur. Co.* (1987)

33.    *Ashbaugh v. Williams* (1987)

# ASSIGNMENT 6

## USE OF THE TABLE OF CASES OF THE
## U.S. SUPREME COURT DIGEST
### (West Publishing Company)

**Method:**

Refer to the Table of Cases of the *U.S. Supreme Court Digest* (West Pub. Co.) and locate the following cases. For each, provide:

(1)     The official (U.S.) citation to the full opinion. Do not provide parallel, memo, cert. or rehearing citations.

(2)     The first-listed Topic and Key Number, if any, immediately following the case citation.

**Example:**

QUESTION:     *Mills v. Duryee*
ANSWER:          (1)     11 U.S. (7 Cranch) 481
                      (2)     Execution 59

**Questions:**

1.     *Aquilino v. United States*

2.     *Buchanan v. City of Litchfield*

3.     *Calder v. Bull*

4.     *DeBlanc v. Texas*

5.     *Erskine v. Hohnbach*

6.     *Ex parte Hagger*

7.     *Fisher v. Shropshire*

8.     *Gomillion v. Lightfoot*

9.     *Huff v. Doyle*

10.  *In Re Loving*

11.  *International Bank v. Sherman*

12.  *Jeter v. Hewitt*

13.  *The Keokuk*

14.  *Kinsella v. Krueger*

15.  *Leib v. Bolton*

16.  *McKimm v. Riddle*

17.  *Omaha Hotel Co. v. Kountze*

18.  *Potts v. Hollon*

19.  *Quicksall v. Michigan*

20.  *Read v. City of Plattsmouth*

21.  *Sarlls v. United States*

22.  *Scott v. Paisley*

23.  *Town of Lyon v. Munson*

24.  *Trbovich v. United Mine Workers of America*

25.  *Urquhart v. Brown*

26.  *United States v. Moseley*

27.  *Villalobos v. United States*

28.  *Willing v. Rinenstock*

29.  *Yee Hem v. United States*

30.  *Zahn v. Board of Public Works of City of Los Angeles*

# ASSIGNMENT 7

## USE OF THE TABLE OF CASES OF THE U.S. SUPREME COURT REPORTS DIGEST, LAWYERS' EDITION

**Method:**

Refer to the Table of Cases of the *U.S. Supreme Court Reports Digest, Lawyers' Edition* (Lawyers' Cooperative Publishing.). Locate the below-listed cases and provide:

(1)     The official (U.S.) citation to the full opinion, if any. Do not provide parallel, memo, cert. or rehearing citations.

(2)     The first-listed Topic and Section Number, if any, immediately following the case citation.

**Example:**

QUESTION:     *Mitchum v. Foster*
ANSWER:     (1)     407 U.S. 225
            (2)     Civil Rights § 22

**Questions:**

1.     *The Adela*

2.     *Boujiois v. Chapman*

3.     *Calder v. Bull*

4.     *Di Piero v. Pennsylvania*

5.     *Ex parte Dainard*

6.     *FHA v. Burr*

7.     *Fisher v. Shropshire*

8.     *Goldsborough v. Orr*

9.     *The Great Republic*

10. *Jenkins v. McKeithen*

11. *The Keokuk*

12. *Kowalski v. Chandler*

13. *Loving v. Virginia*

14. *McDonald v. Magruder*

15. *MacDougall v. Green*

16. *NLRB v. C & C Plywood Corp.*

17. *Ohio ex rel. Lloyd v. Dollison*

18. *Pierce v. Society of the Sisters*

19. *Quinlan v. Green County*

20. *Roberts v. Cay*

21. *Rosenbloom v. Metromedia Inc.*

22. *Scott v. Paisley*

23. *Texas & P.R. Co. v. American Tie and Timber Co,*

24. *Trbovich v. United Mine Workers of America*

25. *The Umbria*

26. *Vachon v. New Hampshire*

27. *Whittington v. Petelow*

28. *Wisconsin v. Yoder*

29. *Yazoo & M.V.R. Co. v. Mullins*

30. *Zartarian v. Billings*

## ASSIGNMENT 8

## USE OF THE TABLE OF CASES OF
## WEST'S MODERN FEDERAL PRACTICE DIGEST, FEDERAL
## PRACTICE DIGEST, 2d,
## FEDERAL PRACTICE DIGEST, 3d, AND
## FEDERAL PRACTICE DIGEST, 4th

**Method:**

Refer to the Table of Cases of the *Modern Federal Practice* Digest, the *Federal Practice Digest, 2d,* the *Federal Practice Digest, 3d* and *the Federal Practice Digest, 4th.* Locate the below-listed cases and provide:

(1)     The citation for each case. Do not cite reversing, affirming, memo, or cert. cases.

(2)     The first-listed Topic and Key Number, if any, immediately following the case citation.

**Example:**

QUESTION:     *McGraw-Edition Co. v. Central Transformer Core.* (1962)

ANSWER:     (1)     308 F.2d 70 (8th Cir. 1962)

(2)     Appeal and Error 198

**Questions:**

1.     *The A.H. Quinby* (1879)

2.     *Alexander v. Silverman* (1973)

3.     *Arna v. Northwestern University* (1986)

4.     *Baldwin Rubber Co. v. Paine & Williams Co.* (1939)

5.     *Caraway v. Califano* (1980)

6.     *Carey v. Settle* (1966)

7.     *Dallas Oil & Gas Co., Matter of* (1981)

8. *In re Chagra* (1965)

9. *Frankel v. Commissioner of Ed.* (1979)

10. *Delesdernier v. O'Rourke & Warren Co.* (1962)

11. *Hayward v. C.I.R.* (1984)

12. *Ferguson v. Cardwell* (1971)

13. *G & W Towing Co. v. Barges CB-I* (1966)

14. *John Doe Corp. v. Miller* (1980)

15. *Iannelli v. Long* (1971)

16. *Meeropol v. Meese* (1986)

17. *Justh v. Holtman* (1965)

18. *Lester v. Isbrandtsen Co.* (1950)

19. *Mack v. 48 Vesey Street Corporation* (1947)

20. *Samimi v. I.N.S.* (1983)

21. *NLRB v. Colten* (1939)

22. *Oy v. Half* (1940)

23. *U.C. Castings Co. v. Knight* (1985)

24. *Petition of Gogate* (1942)

25. *In re Robertson* (1954)

26. *W.R. Grace & Co. v. Pullman, Inc.* (1976)

27. *Rochford v. Volatile* (1970)

28. *S.S. Audrey J. Luckenbach* (1963)

29. *U.S. v. Puchi* ( 1971 )

30. *United States v. Swank* (1971)

31. *Gottshall v. Consolidated Rail Corp.* (1991).

32. *Weaver v. University of Cincinnati* (1992).

33. *Parsons v. Sullivan* (1992).

# ASSIGNMENT 9

## JUDICIAL DEFINITIONS OF VARIOUS WORDS AND PHRASES

**Method:**

Using the three indicated sources, locate a judicial definition of the word or phrase stated in the problem. Give only the name of the first case cited, if any, in each source. If none, state "Not Listed."

**Sources:**    (1)    Words and Phrases (W & P)
    (2)    *Federal Practice Digest, 4th,* (FPD)
    (3)    *U.S. Supreme Court Digest* (West) (WD)

**Example:**

QUESTION:    Fence
ANSWER:    (1)    (W & P) *Bollenbach v. United States*
    (2)    (FPD)    *U.S. v. Rippy*
    (3)    (WD)    *Bollenbach v. United States*

**Questions:**

1. Abnormal

2. Alien

3. Carrying on Business

4. Contemporaneous

5. De Novo

6. Death

7. Discrimination

8. Easement

9. Employee

10. Entrapment

11.   Gratuitous

12.   Highest

13.   Incorporating

14.   Kick-back (or kickback)

15.   Lascivious

16.   Left

17.   Magic Words Doctrine

18.   Mens Rea

19.   Next of Kin

20.   Outlaw

21.   Quorum

22.   Refuses to Answer

23.   Signature

24.   Subrogation

25.   Unusual

26.   Waiver

27.   X-Rays

28.   Ponzi Scheme

29.   Ozark Hillbilly

30.   Merger

# ASSIGNMENT 10

## STATE DIGESTS

**Method:**

Answer the questions using the state digest for your state. Answers to each question will vary according to the state. If your state is Delaware, Nevada, or Utah use the appropriate regional digest.

1. Identify the state digest within your state.

2. Is there an index to your state digest? What is it called? How do you use it to find cases in your state?

3. Describe the methods of supplementation for your state digest?

4. Describe how you update the research you found in your state digest through the advance sheets for the more recent cases?

5. Find the "Table of Cases" volumes for your state digest. What information does it give you for each case?

6. Find the "Words and Phrases" volumes for your state digest. Is there a case that defines the word "person?" If there is more than one case list the earliest case.

7. Look up in the annotated code for your state the law covering inheritance by an adopted person. What claims does an adopted person have on their natural parents' estates? Find a case in your state in the annotations. Look up this case in a west regional or state digest. What is the topic and key number in the West's system that covers this topic?

8. Now take the topic and key number you found in question 7 and find additional cases in your state through your state digest. Now broaden your search with this same topic and key number and see if there are cases in a bordering state. Is there a federal case that deals with this topic?

9. Are federal cases listed in your state digest? Why?

## ASSIGNMENT 11

## THEME AND DRILL PROBLEMS FOR DIGESTS FOR COURT DECISIONS

The problems that follow are designed to acquaint you with the many features and impressive scope of digests. To answer these problems requires analytical thinking on your part. It also often requires you to think like an editor as you try to determine how various words and phrases in an index might provide references to the sources you are researching.

Some hints to help you along the way should make use of the digests almost enjoyable. When the directions ask you to use the most specific digest available, be sure to do so. For example, if the question says it is a U.S. Supreme Court case, use a Supreme Court digest. If it is a federal court case, use a federal digest. If it is a state case, use that state's digest, if available in your library. If the appropriate state digest is unavailable, you must use the decennials or the proper regional digest.

Note also that the problems instruct you to search under a specific Topic and Key Number. Remember that Topics and Key Numbers expand or they are placed under a new Topic in subsequent digests.

Working with the digests provides you with a good opportunity to work on developing proper citation technique through use of *A Uniform System of Citation* ("Blue Book"). Read about the proper order for citations, parallel citations, and spacing. Place the cases you cite as answers in "Blue Book" form.

## THEME PROBLEMS FOR DIGESTS

### Theme Problem I:

A.  QUESTION: In the West publication of the *Brown* decision, 74 S. Ct. 686, two Key Numbers under the topic Constitutional Law are assigned in the headnotes. What two numbers are they?

ANSWER:     Constitutional Law 47, 220

B     Using the Key Numbers in *Brown* assigned to headnote number four and its subsections as a guide, answer the following questions using the most specific digest your library has available:

1. Locate a 1968 U.S. Supreme Court decision which holds that no official student transfer plan of which racial segregation is the inevitable result can stand under the 14th Amendment.

2. Find a 1970 Federal District Court decision that holds that while no student has a constitutional right to play football, no student can be prohibited from doing so solely on the basis of race.

3. Locate a Federal court of Appeals decision in 1972 that holds that where it is possible to determine whether a school is for whites or blacks simply by reference to the racial composition of its faculty and staff, a prima facie case of violation of Equal Protection is made out.

4. Find a 1936 Maryland case that held that a Negro student was entitled to admission to the law school of the state university where the state could furnish "separate but equal" facilities no other way.

C. Using the Topic and Key Number assigned to headnote number one of *Brown* as a start, answer the following questions by referring to the most specific digest available in your library.

1. Find a 1977 Georgia case that holds that a county ordinance seeking to regulate "X- rated" movies through special fees, although justified as being merely a business regulation, will be subject to judicial scrutiny.

2. Find a 1974 U.S. Court of Appeals case where a statute forbidding the acceptance of an unlawful gratuity is being invoked against a former U.S. Senator, hypothetical cases showing possible effects on First Amendment should be ignored.

3. Find a 1975 U.S. Court of Appeals decision that holds that where complaining Library of Congress employees have not pointed out certain rules as due process violations, the Court does not have to scrutinize them.

4. Locate a 1942 South Carolina case which holds that where a law condemns a business for protection of public health, the Court will inquire into the law's necessity.

5.      Cite a 1977 North Dakota case where a putative father challenging an illegitimacy law who did not assert policies that show the law's unconstitutional application to others will have the Court's inquiry limited to his case.

D.      Using the Table of Cases for the most appropriate digest, provide citations for the following cases:

1.      *Vaughn v. Califano* - Federal case. (1977)

2.      *Zorick v. Jones* - Miss. (1966)

3.      *Aaltio v. CB&Q RR* - Minn. (1936)

4.      *Alford v. Butler* - Tenn. (1963)

5.      *Caldwell v. Sturdivant* - Ga. (1923)

**Theme Problem II:**

A.      QUESTION:  *Roe v. Wade*, 93 S. Ct. 705 has one Key Number assigned to headnote 11 and two to headnote 16. List these three Key Numbers.

          ANSWER:    Constitutional Law 82, Abortion 1, Constitutional Law 258.3

B.      Using the Key Number for headnote 11 and its subsections as a starting place, answer the following questions by referring to the most specific digest available in your library.

1.      Find a 1973 Federal District Court case in Connecticut that holds that a statute compelling an unwed mother to appear before a judge, name the putative father and institute a paternity action does not violate the mother's right to privacy.

2.      Cite a 1978 N.J. case that affirms that states may impose stricter standards for the protection of individual rights than the Federal Constitution.

3.      Find a 1978 Federal case from Texas that holds that the family of an extraordinarily talented high school basketball player had the right to assist the player in developing his talents to the fullest.

4. Cite a 1945 Oklahoma case holding that prohibiting the sale of 3.2 beer in establishments that permit dancing is not violative of state constitutions guarantee of individual rights.

5. Cite a 1967 New Hampshire case that held that a statute forbidding parades on streets and public ways without first obtaining a license did not violate First Amendment guarantees.

C. Using whichever of the Key Numbers attached to headnote 16 (and/or its subdivisions) that seems relevant as a starting place, answer the following:

1. Locate a 1977 case that held invalid a Florida statute that authorized abortions only in certified centers and required doctors to sign a stipulation before each operation.

2. Cite a 1977 Nebraska case that upholds a statute making the possession of one pound or less of marijuana a misdemeanor as not violative of equal protection.

3. Cite a 1975 Federal District Court case in Pennsylvania striking down a Pennsylvania statute that requires a woman to get signed permission from her spouse prior to an abortion.

4. Find a Federal Court of Appeals decision coming from Arizona that holds that failure to make intent a part of the crime of possession of an unregistered firearm does not violate due process.

5. Locate a 1978 Iowa case that finds the undefined term "indecent" as a standard of behavior in a statute to be violative of due process.

D. Using the Table of Cases for the most appropriate digest, provide citations for the following cases:

1. *Denneny v. Siegel* - Federal case. (1967)

2. *Quirici v. Freeman* - Cal. (1950)

3. *Hoffman v. Victory Rubber Co.* - Wash. (1922)

4. *Climax Dairy Co. v. Mulder* - Colo. (1925)

5.    *Tresher v. McElroy* - Fla. (1925)

# DRILL PROBLEMS FOR DIGEST

**Instructions:**

A.    For each of the hypotheticals in Section A of each Drill Problem Section, use the indicated *Decennial Digest* and provide:

> (1)    A "yes" or "no" answer to the question.
>
> (2)    The Topic and Key Number under which your answer was found.
>
> (3)    The *Uniform System of Citation* cite form for the case that provides the answer.
>
> NOTE:  If you are unable to locate a specific case that yields the "yes" or "no" answer, locate other Topic and Key Numbers that offer cases of interest.

B.    In Subsection B of each Drill Problem Section, use the case table in the appropriate set of Decennial Digests to complete the citations.

**Drill Problem I:**

A.    Topics and Key Numbers:

**Questions:**

> 1.    Use Third Decennial. A petition was filed with the Minnesota Board of Law Examiners seeking the disbarment of an attorney for alleged misconduct in signing a will as a witness after the testatrix had died.  Was the evidence of this alleged misconduct sufficient to sustain the charge?
>
> 2.    Use Fourth Decennial. Plaintiff sued for rent under a written lease. After a finding for the defendant, plaintiff contended that the court lacked jurisdiction since the order had been entered before return of proof of service had been filed. In New Hampshire does failure to file the return deny the court jurisdiction?

3. Use Fifth Decennial. Relying on the Mississippi statute which provided that one was presumed dead if absent for seven years without having been heard from, Freda, whose first husband had been absent and not heard from for more than seven years, married Bill. Subsequent to Freda's marriage to Bill it was discovered that Freda's first husband was alive. Was the marriage of Freda and Bill void?

4. Use Sixth Decennial. A San Francisco attorney entered into a contingent fee contract with a client. The contract had the effect of providing additional compensation if a cross- complaint was filed and successfully defended. Does this make the contract illegal, unfair or inequitable?

5. Use Seventh Decennial. The treasurer of a union local entered into a scheme with the other members of the union's executive board whereby he sold union property and pocketed part of the proceeds. In California does pocketing part of proceeds from sale of realty belonging to union constitute embezzlement?

B. Table of Cases:

**Questions:**

1. Dicennials or Regional Digests

    (a) *Cain v. Mead County* (1929)

    (b) *Escobar v. State* (1965)

    (c) *Groover v. Terrell* (1919)

    (d) *Idol v. Street* (1951)

    (e) *Lee County v. James* (1937)

2. U.S. Supreme Court Citations

    (a) *Chemgas v. Tynan*

    (b) *Ghio v. Moore*

    (c) *Moelle v. Sherwood*

(d)    *Reaves v. Ainsworth*

(e)    *Urquhart v. Brown*

## Drill Problem II:

A.    Topics and Key Numbers:

## Questions:

1.    Use *Third Decennial*. A city in Arkansas sued to recover possession of a block of land which the city alleged had been dedicated to public use. A plat of the land had been filed in the office of the Recorder of Deeds. The block in question was designated "Franklin Square," but was not put to public use nor ever accepted by the City Council as a public place. Did the marking of the block as a "square" constitute an implied dedication of the land to the city?

2.    Use *Fourth Decennial*. In a suit for specific performance of a contract to sell certain real estate in California, evidence showed that in 1921, the contract was entered into at a purchase price of $3,000, of which $2,853.32 was to be paid in installments. On July 28, 1927, plaintiff tendered $1400 to defendant and demanded that she execute and deliver a conveyance to him. She refused. In an action for specific performance in the State of California, is tender of money by purchaser, without payment, sufficient to show good faith and diligence?

3.    Use *Fifth Decennial*. A tenant sued his landlord for injuries sustained when he injured his hand on the porcelain handle of a faucet over the kitchen sink in his Chicago apartment. He rented the apartment under a month to month tenancy. The janitor of the building had allegedly promised to repair the faucet, but there was no evidence to show any promise by the landlord to make repairs prior to commencement of the tenancy. Was the landlord liable?

4.    Use *Sixth Decennial*. A woman filed a complaint against an attorney with the Monmouth County, New Jersey, Ethics and Grievance Committee. He retaliated by starting a malicious prosecution action against her. May an attorney predicate a malicious prosecution action on the filing of such a complaint?

5.    Use *Seventh Decennial*. An actress entered into a contract with an

agency to be her exclusive representative for a period of five years. Under the contract she was to pay the agency 10% of her earnings. Simultaneously the agency allegedly made an oral agreement to pay 5% of her earnings to another agent to whom she was already under contract. In New York, does the statute of frauds bar enforcement of such an oral agreement made in conjunction with an artist's exclusive agency contract?

B.      Table of Cases:

## Questions:

1.      Decennials or Regional Digests:

   (a)      *Carse v. Marsh* (1922)

   (b)      *Feverchak v. Hiatt* (1948)

   (c)      *Haggerty v. Clement* (1940)

   (d)      *James River Bank v. Hansen*

   (e)      *Locigno v. City of Chicago* (1961)

2.      U.S. Supreme Court Citations

   (a)      *Ex parte Dainard*

   (b)      *Hanna v. Maas*

   (c)      *Neil v. Biggers*

   (d)      *Scott v. Paisley*

   (e)      *Vachon v. New Hampshire*

# Chapter 8

# CONSTITUTIONAL LAW

## ASSIGNMENT 1

## UNITED STATES CONSTITUTION

**Sources:**      *United States Code Annotated* (Constitution volumes)
*United States Code Service* (Constitution volumes)
*The Constitution of the United States of America* (Library of Congress, 1996)

**Method:**

Briefly answer the questions, using one of the above source materials. List the applicable article, section, and clause of the Constitution, and if the question involves judicial interpretation of a constitutional provision, cite a case in point.

**Questions and Answers:**

1.    QUESTION:      The City of Burbank sought enforcement of its city ordinance prohibiting take-off by jet aircraft from an airport between the hours of 11:00 p.m. and 7:00 a.m. Lockheed Air Terminal, Inc. resisted. What result? (Use *Constitution of the United States of America*.)

2.    QUESTION:      Is a member of Congress eligible to hold a commission in the Armed Forces during his continuance in office as a Congressman? (Use *Constitution of the United of America* or U.S.C.S. or U.S.C.A.)

3.    QUESTION:    What House of Congress has the sole power to try all impeachments? (Use *Constitution of the United States of America* or U.S.C.S or U.S.C.A.)

4.    QUESTION:    What vote is required for a House of Congress to expel a member? (Use *Constitution of the United States of America* or U.S.C.S. or U.S.C.A.)

5.    QUESTION:    If the President vetoes a bill and returns it to the House of Congress in which it originated, what formalities are necessary to override the veto and make the bill a law? (Use *Constitution of the United States of America* or U.S.C.S. or U.S.C.A.)

6.    QUESTION:    For what Federal officials must the President have the advise and consent of the Senate to effect their appointment to Federal office? (Use *Constitution of the United States of America* or U.S.C.S. or U.S.C.A.)

7.    QUESTION:    What limitations does the Constitution provide as to the formation of new States of the Union? (Use *Constitution of the United States of America* or U.S.C.S. or U.S.C.A.)

8.    QUESTION:    What constitutional provision regulates interstate compacts? (Use *Constitution of the United States of America* or U.S.C.S. or U.S.C.A

9.    QUESTION:    Are treaties the supreme law of the land? (Use *Constitution of the United States of America* or U.S.C.S. or U.S.C.A.)

10.    QUESTION:    If a Vice President assumes the office of President in the first year of his

predecessor's elected term, may he seek reelection on his own a second time?(Use *Constitution of the United States of America or* U.S.C.S. or U.S.C.A.)

11.  QUESTION:  Under what constitutional authority does the Supreme Court act in reviewing the judgments and decrees of the supreme courts of the several states when federal questions are involved? (Use *Constitution of the United States of America* or U.S.C.S. or U.S.C.A.)

12.  QUESTION:  Does Congress have power to impose higher taxes in one state than in another? (Use *Constitution of the United States of America* or U.S.C.S. or U.S.C.A.)

13.  QUESTION:  For what type of cases does the Supreme Court of the United States have original jurisdiction? (Use *Constitution of the United States of America* or U.S.C.S. or U.S.C.A.)

14.  QUESTION:  Every bill passed by both Houses must be presented to the President before it becomes law. Two courses of action by the President are prescribed by the Constitution, either of which will result in the bill becoming law. What are they? (Use U.S.C.S.)

15.  QUESTION:  A Wisconsin compulsory school attendance law requires that Amish children attend high school.  Parents of Amish children challenge the statute on the ground that the statute is contrary their religious beliefs. What result? (Use *Constitution of the United States of America*

16.  QUESTION:  A juvenile is charged with delinquency which may result in commitment. The

parents and child are unable to employ counsel. Do they have a right to court-appointed counsel? (Use *Constitution of the United States of* America.)

17. QUESTION: Who determines when Presidential disability exists under the 25th Amendment? (Use *Constitution oft he United States of America* or U.S.C.S.)

18. QUESTION: May a state grant property tax exemptions to religious organizations for religious properties used solely for worship? (Use *Constitution of the United States of America* to find case cite.)

19. QUESTION: May Federal judges be removed from office by impeachment? Cite only the correct constitutional provision. (Use *Constitution of the United States of America*.)

20. QUESTION: The Constitution authorizes the removal of a President by impeachment, brought by the House of Representatives and tried by the Senate. What federal official presides over the trial? (Use *Constitution of the United States of America* or U.S.C.S. or U.S.C.A.)

# ASSIGNMENT 2

## UNITED STATES CONSTITUTION

**Method:**

Using the tables and information contained in *The Constitution of the United States of America* (Library of Congress, 1996) answer the following questions.

**Questions and Answers:**

1. QUESTION: How many amendments to the Constitution have not been ratified after being submitted to the states?

2. QUESTION: What is the subject of the most recent proposed amendment to the constitution which was submitted to the states for ratification and failed to pass?

3. QUESTION: What is the subject matter of the proposed 28th Amendment to the Constitution?

4. QUESTION: In 1918 the Supreme Court held unconstitutional a statute prohibiting interstate shipment of articles made by child labor. What was the law and the case?

5. QUESTION: What case held unconstitutional the provisions of the immigration and Naturalization Act of 1952, which provided for revocation of citizenship of those who had voted in a foreign election

6. QUESTION: The Internal Revenue Code of 1954 had a provision which required gamblers to declare their gambling income. These provisions were held not to prevent the assertion of one's privilege against self-incrimination. Which cases held this?

7.    QUESTION:    What case held unconstitutional the section of the Voting Rights Act Amendments of 1970 that set the minimum age of 18 in state and local elections?

8.    QUESTION:    *Shapiro v. Thompson,* 394 U.S. 618 (1969), held what Act of Congress to be unconstitutional?

9.    QUESTION:    In what case did the Supreme Court hold that a Virginia statute which prohibited interracial marriages was unconstitutional?

10.   QUESTION:    What 1824 case held that an Ohio statute levying a tax on the Bank of the United States was unconstitutional?

11.   QUESTION:    What 1956 case held that an indigent defendant is entitled to a free copy of the entire transcript of his criminal trial under some circumstances?

12.   QUESTION:    What justices concurred separately in the 1961 *Cramp v. Board of Public Instructions* decision which held unconstitutional a law requiring state and local employees to swear that they never lent support to the Communist Party?

13.   QUESTION:    *Gideon v. Wainwright,* 372 U.S. 335 (1963), overruled what prior case?

14.   QUESTION:    *Wolf v. Colorado*, 338 U.S. 25 (1949), was overruled in part by what 1961 case?

15.   QUESTION:    *West Coast Hotel Co. v. Parrish,* 300 U.S. 379 (1937), overruled what case?

# ASSIGNMENT 3

## COMPARISON OF STATE CONSTITUTIONS

**Sources:**     The Constitution of the states to which reference is made in each question.

*Index-Digest of State Constitutions* (Legislative Drafting Fund of Columbia University, 2d ed., 1959 with 1971 cumulative supplement).

## Method:

Briefly answer the questions and cite the applicable constitutional provision.

**Note to Instructors:**     Instructors may wish to tell students to use relevant state constitutions directly, instead of the *Index-Digest.*

## Questions and Answers:

1.  QUESTION:     May divorces be granted by private, local or special law in:
    Alabama
    Indiana
    Nevada

2.  QUESTION:     May a person under guardianship vote in:
    Arizona
    Idaho
    Minnesota

3.  QUESTION:     May legitimation be authorized by local, private or special law in:
    California
    Texas
    Wyoming

4.  QUESTION:     Is the property of public libraries exempt from taxation in:
    California
    Oklahoma

5.    QUESTION:    Is a state lottery legal in New York?

6.    QUESTION:    Do the Nevada and Utah state constitutions define periods of emergency resulting from disasters caused by enemy attack?

7.    QUESTION:    What constitutional clauses provide a method of invoking initiative and referendum in:
California
Michigan
Nevada

8.    QUESTION:    Are canals treated as public highways in Arkansas?

9.    QUESTION:    Does the Louisiana state constitution provide for the payment of a pension to a surviving spouse and minor children of law enforcement officers killed while engaged in the direct apprehension of persons during course of performance of duties?

10.    QUESTION:    Are military records and relics preserved in the office of the adjutant-general in Idaho?

11.    QUESTION:    May absconding debtors be imprisoned in Washington and Utah?

12.    QUESTION:    Are sheriffs commissioned by the governors in Arkansas and Delaware?

13.    QUESTION:    Is polygamy expressly prohibited by constitutional provision in Utah and Oklahoma?

14.    QUESTION:    Are perpetuities allowable for eleemosynary purposes in Nevada?

15.    QUESTION:    Are retrospective laws permissible in:
Colorado, Tennessee, Texas.

16.    QUESTION:    How are claims brought against the state in: Arizona, Washington, Wisconsin?

17.   QUESTION:        What constitutes a woman's separate
                       property in: Alabama, Michigan, Utah?

18.   QUESTION:        In case of suicide how does property
                       descend in:  Colorado, Delaware, Texas?.

19.   QUESTION:        What does the Michigan constitution
                       provide with respect to findings of fact in
                       worker's compensation proceedings?

20.   QUESTION:        What does the Wyoming constitution
                       provide with respect to the make up of
                       Congressional districts?

# ASSIGNMENT 4

## STATE CONSTITUTIONS -- INDEXES

**Sources:**

The general index to the appropriate state statutes, index to the constitution, topical analysis of separate articles, and notes to the decisions of each state to which reference is made.

**Method:**

Using the above sources, cite the applicable constitutional provision for each question below.

**Questions and Answers:**

1. QUESTION: Cite the Maine constitutional provision dealing with construction of buildings for industrial use.

2. QUESTION: The Maine legislature's authority to insure Maine veterans' mortgage loans up to eighty percent.

3. QUESTION: The Maine Constitution includes a provision which amends the apportionment of senatorial districts beginning in 1983.

4. QUESTION: Cite the Wyoming constitutional article dealing with changing the names of persons or places.

5. QUESTION: Is there a limitation on municipal indebtedness for the purpose of building sewers in Wyoming?

6. QUESTION: Does the U.S. government have jurisdiction over Indian land in Wyoming?

7.    QUESTION:            Does the schedule of the Tennessee
                           Constitution of 1870 provide for the
                           appointment of a state reporter?

8.    QUESTION:            In Tennessee, can the size of an existing
                           county be reduced to less than 275 square
                           miles?

9.    QUESTION:            Which section of the Tennessee
                           Constitution deals with the pay and
                           allowances for members of the General
                           Assembly?

# ASSIGNMENT 5

## STATE CONSTITUTIONS -- CONSTRUCTION

**Method:**

Using bound volumes, bound supplements, specific pamphlet supplements, pocket parts, and general pamphlet supplements to the appropriate state statutes, cite the cases and answer the questions given below.

**Questions and Answers:**

1.      QUESTION:      With reference to your answer of Question 1, Assignment 4 above, cite the Maine authority fixing the minimum limit on percentage of voters who may authorize issuance of municipal bonds, below which the Legislature may not go.

2.      QUESTION:      Cite a 1975 Maine authority construing Article IV, part 1, section 8 of the Maine Constitution.

3.      QUESTION:      With reference to your answer to the same section of the Wyoming Constitution given in your answer to Question 4, Assignment 4, cite a Wyoming case holding that because a statute applies only to one city it is not necessarily unconstitutional as special legislation.

4.      QUESTION:      Article IX, sec. 1 of the Wyoming Constitution has a section which discusses the position of inspector of mines. In the "cross references" annotation to the section, two cases are listed. When were these two cases decided? Cite the older case.

5.      QUESTION:      Cite a 1998 case that indicated the state is allowed to adjudicate Indian water rights. (Wind River Indian Reservation)

6.    QUESTION:    Cite the case which discusses power dam construction on former Indian lands.

7.    QUESTION:    With reference to the Sixth Amendment of the United States Constitution, cite the Tennessee case holding that a defendant's right to a speedy trial was not denied right to speedy trial where he was tried within eight months after he was arrested on charges of buying and possessing unstamped liquor, especially in view of the fact that he was not confined in jail prior to trial.

8.    QUESTION:    With reference to the same section of the Tennessee Constitution given in your answer to Question 8, Assignment 4 above, cite the 1917 Tennessee case indicating whether the size of a county of less than 500 square miles could be further reduced.

9.    QUESTION:    With reference to your answer to Question 9, Assignment 4 above, cite the 1974 Tennessee case which discusses the state general assembly.

10.    QUESTION:    When (if ever) was that section of the New Mexico Constitution dealing with the right to bear arms most recently amended?

# ASSIGNMENT 6

## THEME PROBLEMS AND DRILL PROBLEMS

**Theme Problem I and Answers:**

1.  QUESTION:    What parts of the U.S. Constitution does *Brown v. Board of Education* (347 U.S. 483) discuss?

2.  QUESTION:    Name four places where one could locate those sections.

3.  QUESTION:    What is the advantage of an annotated constitution?

4.  QUESTION:    Using U.S.C.A., find discussion of the *Brown* decision under the Equal Protection point of the 14th Amendment. Under what heading and number does it appear?

5.  QUESTION:    How can one get into such specialized areas when there are so many cases digested?

6.  QUESTION:    Using U.S.C.S., find discussion of the *Brown* decision under the Equal Protection Clause of the 14th Amendment. Under what heading and number does it appear?

7.  QUESTION:    Using U.S.C.S., where could one find cases on racial discrimination in education?

8.  QUESTION:    Using U.S.C.S., does the bound volume cite any Annotations on the topic of Brown?

9.  QUESTION:    Using U.S.C.S., if one wanted to find related law review articles, where could one look?

## Theme Problem II and Answers:

1.   QUESTION:   What part of the Constitution does *Roe v. Wade* (410 U.S. 113) rely upon?

2.   QUESTION:   Name four places where you could find the text involved.

3.   QUESTION:   What would be the advantage of using an annotated constitution?

4.   QUESTION:   Using the U.S.C.S. Constitution volumes to answer Questions 4-7, where can one find discussion of the *Roe* case under the heading of Abortions -- generally?

5.   QUESTION:   How many places would you have to check to be sure you have all current cases on the subject?

6.   QUESTION:   Using the Constitution volumes of U.S.C.S. for Questions 8-11, where in the notes could you find the *Roe* decision digested as a criminal matter?

7.   QUESTION:   Where could one find related law review articles?

8.   QUESTION:   Cite a relevant Annotation.

9.   QUESTION:   What does the abbreviation "LC" mean?

10.   QUESTION:   Contrast the information found through U.S.C.A. and U.S.C.S.; which is more useful and why?

11.   QUESTION:   Does your home state have a constitutional provision on abortion? If so, cite and state its status.

**Drill Problem I and Answers:**

Use the Constitution as printed in the U.S.C.A. or the U.S.C.S. to answer the following:

1.      QUESTION:      What article and section of the Constitution deals with the power of Congress to declare war?

2.      QUESTION:      What provision empowers Congress to define what constitutes piracy and to set punishments for it?

3.      QUESTION:      What provision prohibits states from keeping ships of war without the consent of Congress?

4.      QUESTION:      Which provision guarantees a trial by jury in criminal cases? Locate a 1953 decision from the Sixth Circuit which holds that the elements of a constitutional jury trial that require 12 jurors and a unanimous verdict are procedural and not jurisdictional.

5.      QUESTION:      What provision gives Congress the power to grant copyrights?

**Drill Problem II and Answers:**

Use the Constitution as printed in U.S.C.A. or U.S.C.S. to answer the following:

1.      QUESTION:      Which Amendment prevents a criminal defendant from having to face the same charges twice?

2.      QUESTION:      Cite a 1978 federal decision from an Alabama case holding that intent is a necessary element in an action for racial gerrymandering under the XV Amendment.

3.    QUESTION:        Where is it specified that two witnesses are needed to convict a person of treason?

4.    QUESTION:        What provision prevents a religious test from ever being applied as a requirement for any office in the federal government?

## Drill Problem III and Answers:

Use the Constitution as printed in U.S.C.A. or U.S.C.S. to answer the following:

1.    QUESTION:        What part of the Constitution mandates the taking of a national census at 10 year intervals?

2.    QUESTION:        What provisions deal with taxation of native Americans?

3.    QUESTION:        Where is the pardon power of the President created?

4.    QUESTION:        Which clause of the Constitution deals with habeas corpus?

# Chapter 9

# FEDERAL LEGISLATION

## ASSIGNMENT 1

## FEDERAL LEGISLATION - PARALLEL REFERENCE TABLES: U.S.C.

**Method:**

Using the parallel reference tables of the *United States Code,* the *United States Code Annotated,* or the *United States Code Service,* give the U.S.C. citation for each of the public laws.

**Questions:**

1. 92-230

2. 93-387

3. 91-586

4. 90-619 § 1.

5. 89-29

6. 86-591

7. 94-209

8. 87-824

9. 97-62

10. 98-167

11. 95-127

12. 106-116

## ASSIGNMENT 2

## FEDERAL LEGISLATION - PARALLEL REFERENCE TABLES: U.S.C.C.A.N.

**Method:**

Using the Table of Classifications in the *U.S. Code Congressional and Administrative News*, give the U.S.C. citation for each of the following public laws.

**Questions:**

1.  89-360

2.  89-586

3.  89-615

4.  89-771

5.  90-66

6.  90-330

7.  90-498

8.  90-597

9.  91-5

10. 91-233

11. 91-300

12. 95-233

13. 97-62

14. 97-275

15. 98-81

16.     98-217

17.     99-258

18.     100-174

19.     100-633

20.     100-695

21.     101-412

22.     102-183

23.     102-500

24.     102-307

25.     102-242

26.     101-646

# ASSIGNMENT 3

## UNITED STATES CODE CONGRESSIONAL AND ADMINISTRATIVE NEWS: USE OF THE INDEX TO LOCATE ACTS

**Method:**

Using the index to the *U.S. Code Congressional and Administrative News,* give the number of the Senate or House bill, the Public Law number and the approval date of the Act.

**Questions:**

A.    1969 volumes:

1.    Providing for a national center on educational media and materials for the handicapped.

2.    Protection of children from hazardous toys.

3.    Establishing a national policy for the environment.

4.    Establishment of a Commission on Government Procurement.

5.    Increasing the rates of dependency and indemnity compensation payable to widows of veterans.

B.    1970 volumes:

1.    Special packaging to protect children from ingestion of poisons.

2.    Disposition of geothermal steam resources.

3.    Prohibiting the movement in interstate commerce of "sored" horses.

4.    Rate of duty on parts of stethoscopes.

5.    Continuation of the International Coffee Agreement Act of 1968.

C.    1980 volumes:

    1.    Establishing national poison prevention week.

    2.    Providing for construction, reconstruction and renovation of academic facilities.

    3.    Regulation of saccharin.

    4.    Prevention of kidnapping by parents.

    5.    Dealing with insect, fungus, and rodent control.

D.    1986 volumes:

    1.    Reporting hours of employment of batboys and batgirls.

    2.    Relating to actions against the United States to quiet title.

    3.    Establishing privacy of electronic communications.

    4.    Designing system of fair debt collection practices for attorneys.

    5.    Establishing national marketing quotas for tobacco' and tobacco products.

E.    1988 volumes:

    1.    Protecting and managing archeological resources.

    2.    Price supports for the cotton industry.

    3.    Regulating use of degradable plastic ring carriers.

    4.    Health and accident insurance for temporary federal employees.

    5.    Establishing a fishing agreement with the Soviet Union.

F.    1990 volumes:

    1.    An act to augment and improve the quality of international data on Foreign Direct Investment.

2.    Establishing a conservation area in Southern Nevada containing Red Rock Canyon..

3.    Establishing an office of Minority Health within the Office of the Assistant Secretary for Health.

4.    Requiring F.C.C. to prescribe standards for commercial broadcast licensees with respect to time devoted to commercials in conjunction with children's television programs.

G.    1991 volumes:

1.    Determining the feasibility of establishing a cultural center in Oklahoma to showcase the historical culture of the Native American Heritage in Oklahoma.

2.    Improving the research development and information dissemination through a national research center to eliminate illiteracy by the year 2000.

3.    Providing financial assistance to private organizations to conduct three-year demonstration projects for the benefit of small business concerns owned and controlled by women.

H.    1992 volumes:

1.    Defining pregnancy success rates and developing a model program for the certification of embryo laboratories.

2.    Issuing 500,000 one dollar coins with a design emblematic of the White House.

3.    Publishing a list of nations whose nations or vessels conduct large-scale driftnet fishing beyond the exclusive economic zone of any nation.

# ASSIGNMENT 4

## LOCATING A RECENT STATUTE IN THE U.S. CODE
## BY USE OF THE INDEX

**Sources:**     *United States Code, 2000 Edition*
*United States Code Annotated*
*United States Code Service*

## Method:
(1)     Briefly answer the question.
(2)     Use any of the above sources and cite the relevant title and section of the *United States Code* and the latest *Statutes at Large.*

## Questions:

1.     What is the maximum penalty for violation of the labeling requirement of the Public Health Cigarette Smoking Act of 1969?

2.     Who fixes the per annum rates of basic pay of positions on the National Zoological Park police force?

3.     Is the Secretary of Agriculture authorized to eradicate the golden nematode?

4.     May Coast Guard warrant officers be temporarily promoted to higher warrant officer grades?

5.     Are the natives of the Pribilof Islands entitled by law to receive free dental care from the United States government.

6.     Can U.S. Customs implement assessments of imported cotton?

7.     May the Secretary of the Smithsonian Institution authorize the Employment of aliens?

8.     Is there support for a system in each state to protect the human rights of people with developmental disabilities?

9.     Geothermal leases are for a primary term of how many years?

10. Can instructors of the National Guard use public buildings for their offices?

11. How many members are authorized for the National Advisory Committee on Oceans and Atmosphere?

12. May the Paralyzed Veterans of America promote the candidacy of a person for public office?

13. The United States Postal Service was established as an independent establishment of which branch of the U.S. government?

14. May an employee of the Capitol Guide Service accept a gratuity for his official services?

15. Can the Secretary of State accept money and property as gifts to carry out the purposes of the Center for Cultural and Technical Interchange between East and West?

16. Is California considered a Colorado River Basin State under provisions of the Colorado River Basin Project Act?

17. Under provisions of the Federal Contested Elections Act, must service of the notice of contest upon contestee be made only by delivering a copy to him personally?

# ASSIGNMENT 5

## TABLES OF POPULAR NAMES OF FEDERAL ACTS

**Sources:**    *United States Code*, 2000 edition, Index of Acts Cited by Popular Name.
*United States Code Service*, Lawyers' Edition. Tables. (2004)
*United States Code Annotated*, General Index. (2008)
*Shepard's Acts and Cases by Popular Names.* (1999).

**Method:**

(1)    Using source No. 1 above, give the citation to the first Statutes at Large enactment and to the U.S. Code, by title and first section, as well as the page number of the table where the Act is located.

(2)    Using sources 2 and 3 above, indicate only the page on which the Act is located in each source.

(3)    Using source 4 above, list the first reference which is provided.

**Questions:**

1.    Age Discrimination in Employment Act of 1967.

2.    Commodity Credit Corporation Charter Act.

3.    Environmental Education Act.

4.    Export Apple and Pear Act.

5.    Federal Contested Election Act.

6.    Gambling Devices Act of 1962.

7.    Handicapped Children's Early Education Assistance Act.

8.    National Portrait Gallery Act.

9.    National Trails System Act.

10.    Newspaper Preservation Act.

11.    Radiation Control for Health and Safety Act of 1968.

12.    Service Contract Act of 1965.

13.    Special Drawing Rights Act.

14.     Standard Reference Data Act.

# ASSIGNMENT 6

## FEDERAL LEGISLATION - CODE ANNOTATIONS

**Method:**

Each of the problems below contains a reference to a particular title and section of the *United States Code.* Each such section has been interpreted by the courts. Annotations on a case interpreting a particular section will follow that section in the *United States Code Annotated.* Using these annotations, answer the questions in the problems below. Cite a case supporting your answer.

**Questions:**

1. Categories of priorities for visas for potential immigrants to this country are set out in 8 U.S.C. Sec. 1153. Subsection (a)(3) gives the third priority to immigrants who are members of the professions. Who bears the burden of proof with respect to a third preference visa?

2. The hunting of migratory birds, except as provided by regulation, is outlawed by 16 U.S.C. Sec. 703. Is the red-tailed hawk a migratory bird?

3. A remedy is provided by 25 U.S.C. Sec. 229 for U.S. citizens who have suffered injuries to their property at the hands of an Indian belonging to a tribe in "amity" with the United States. What constitutes "amity" as it is used in this section?

4. All citizens of the U.S. are given the same right to buy and sell property as the white citizen has by 42 U.S.C. Sec. 1982. Has this section ever been held to apply to a cemetery lot?

5. Voting qualifications which are designed to deny citizens the right to vote on account of race are prohibited by 42 U.S.C. Sec. 1973. Has this section ever been given retroactive effect?

6. Peonage in the United States was abolished by 42 U.S.C. Sec. 1994. Would that provision outlaw assignment of attorneys to represent indigents without compensation?

7. Discrimination and segregation in public places are prohibited by 42 U.S.C. Sec. 2000a. Would this prohibition apply to a skating rink?

8. Those persons who may be punished as principals for violations of federal criminal statutes are set out in 18 U.S.C. Sec. 2. Could an officer who agreed to protect a criminal be punished as a principal?

9. Is laches likely to be a good defense to a charge of conspiracy under 18 U.S.C. Sec. 371?

10. It is provided by 28 U.S.C. Sec. 2246 that on an application for a writ of habeas corpus, evidence may be taken by deposition. What law governs the taking of such a deposition?

# ASSIGNMENT 7

## USE OF TABLES FROM FORMER TITLES OF U.S. CODE TO PRESENT TITLE

**Source:**      *United States Code Service* Tables volume or the table before each title in the *United States Code Service.*

**Method:**

Refer to U.S.C.S. Titles Tables. The problems relate to former sections. Give either the current section number of the revised title or the present status of the former section.

**Questions:**

1.    14a, T. 35

2.    526, T. 34

3.    630h, T. 5

4.    1014, T. 31

5.    3335, T. 39

6.    154, T. 35

7.    3572, T. 39

8.    104, T. 10

9.    324, T. 44

10.   32, T.17

11.   282, T. 44

12.   11, T. 17

13.   216, T. 17

14.     109, T. 35

15.     118a, T. 35

# ASSIGNMENT 8

## THEME PROBLEMS AND DRILL PROBLEMS

**Theme Problem I:**

A.      18 U.S.C. sec. 245 proscribes willful interference with anyone's right to a public education on the basis of race. Using the *U.S.C.*, locate that provision and answer the following:

    1.      What was the Public Law number of this legislation?

    2.      Give its Statutes at Large citation.

    3.      What is the fine imposed if bodily injury results?

    4.      If you own and occupy a home with four rooms for hire, are you bound by the law in renting the other units?

B.      Using *U.S.C.A.*, find the same provision and answer the following:

    1.      Have any cases been decided under Sec. 245?

    2.      Cite a case that involved threats to a presidential candidate.

    3.      Has Title 18 been enacted into positive law?

C.      Using *U.S.C.S.*, find the same provision and answer the following:

    1.      Into what four sets does it give you research entry?

    2.      Does 18 *U.S.C.* Sec. 245 create a civil cause of action? Cite a case.

    3.      Does *U.S.C.A.* or *U.S.C.S.* seem more useful? Why?

D.      The 93rd Congress, 2nd Session, passed legislation that all children, regardless of race, color, sex, or national origin, are entitled to equal educational opportunities in the public schools. Find this legislation and answer the following using the appropriate *U.S. Statutes at Large* volume.

    1.      What is the short title of this Act?

2. What is the name and citation of the larger Act of which it is a part?

3. What was the bill number of the Act?

4. Where is Title II codified in *U.S.C.*?

**Theme Problem II:**

A. The plaintiffs and intervenor in *Roe v. Wade* appealed to the U.S. Supreme Court under 28 U.S.C. Sec. 1253. Examine that provision in the *U.S.C.* and answer the following:

1. What was the *U.S. Statutes at Large* citation for this legislation?

2. Where would one look for related sections on writs?

3. Where else in the title is this section referred to?

4. What are the appendices to Title 287?

B. Using *U.S.C.A.*, look up the same provision and answer the following:

1. What Key Numbers apply?

2. Where are cases on the question of "mootness" noted?

3. Where are cases on the Interstate Commerce Commission noted?

C. Using *U.S.C.S.*, look up the same provision and answer these questions:

1. Cite a law review article by Rosenberg on this topic.

2. To what two sets of forms are you given citations?

3. Where are cases on the order of a single judge court noted?

D. Compare and contrast the advantages of the three tools used above.

E. The 94th Congress, 1st Session, passed legislation which forbade any officer or employee of the United States to coerce anyone to have an abortion. Find that legislation using the appropriate U.S. Statutes at Large volume and answer the following:

1.  What is the name and citation of the act?

2.  What was its Senate bill number?

3.  Where will the section on coercion appear in *U.S.C.*?

## Theme Problem III:

A. What is the provision of the *U.S.C.* which deals with the adequate representation of criminal defendants through authorizing each U.S. District Court to draw up a plan?

B. Turn to that provision in *U.S.C.* and answer the following:

  1.  What is the maximum total amount an appointed attorney may receive in a felony case?

  2.  What was the *U.S. Statutes at Large* Act upon which this section is based?

  3.  What was the effective date of the 1974 amendment?

C. Using *U.S.C.A.,* locate this provision and answer the following:

  1.  What Key Numbers will lead to relevant cases?

  2.  Does the pocket part contain new text?

D. Using *U.S.C.S.,* locate the same provision and answer the following:

  1.  Cite a relevant textbook.

  2.  Find a case that decides if the "expert services" made available under subsection 18(e) comprehend psychiatric assistance.

E. Compare and contrast *U.S.C., U.S.C.A.,* and *U.S.C.S.* as to how easy you find them to use.

F. The 91st Congress, 2nd Session, passed legislation that changed the name of the D.C. Legal Aid Agency and redefined its structure and function. Find that legislation using the appropriate U.S. Statutes at Large volume and answer the following:

1.        What is the title and citation of the act of which it is a part?

2.        Which title of the act deals with the Public Defender Service?

3.        Where will these provisions be codified?

## Drill Problem I:

A.        Using either the *U.S.C.,* *U.S.C.A.,* or *U.S.C.S.,* answer the following:

        1.        Where in the Code would one find the penalty for the forgery of a passport?

        2.        Where in the Code is the law affecting the issuance of commercial licenses by the Nuclear Regulatory Commission?

        3.        What section of the Code gives the sentence for a U.S. ship captain who voluntarily surrenders his ship to a pirate?

        4.        What section of the Code requires state legislatures and officers to declare allegiance to the Constitution of the United States?

        5.        Where in the Code does it calculate the average rate of interest of the reserves of a life insurance company?

B.        Using any of the popular name tables (*Shepard's,* *U.S.C.,* *U.S.C.A.* or *U.S.C.S.*), locate the correct citation for the following (it may be necessary to consult more than one):

        1.        Menominee Restoration Act

        2.        Davis-Bacon Act

        3.        Child Health Act of 1967

        4.        Maritime Security Act of 1996

        5.        American Fire Act

C.        For each of the questions in this section, provide:

(1)      The Public Law (or Chapter) number and *Statutes at Large* citation for the original legislation described.

(2)      The location of the legislation in the *U.S.C.* (Note: If it has not been codified, write "none." If it has been codified in several Code locations, list the citation for the earliest part of the Act codified.)

     a.     What 1975 act provides indemnity for creative works that are displayed in exhibitions?

     b.     What act passed by the 90th Congress prescribes penalties for the violation of certain federally protected rights of an individual?

     c.     What act passed by the 93rd Congress enables females to participate in National Little League baseball?

     d.     What act passed by the 85th Congress authorizes construction of the U.S.S. Arizona Memorial?

     e.     What act passed by the 93rd Congress provides financial assistance to prevent child abuse?

**Drill Problem II:**

A.     Using *U.S.C., U.S.C.A.,* or *U.S.C.S.,* answer the following:

     1.     What are the factors determining whether a particular piece of work could be reproduced under the "fair use" doctrine?

     2.     What section of the code declares United States cooperation with other countries in the control of narcotics?

     3.     What section of the code specifies the age limits of those liable for training and service in a military draft?

     4.     What is the punishment for the disclosure of information involving U.S. communication of intelligence to aid a foreign country?

5.      What is the law that prescribes compensation for federal court librarians?

B.      Using any of the popular name tables, locate the correct citation for the following:

1.      Bloody Bill Act

2.      Shipbuilding Act

3.      Saccharin Study and Labelling Act of 1983

4.      Refugee Relief Act of 1953

5.      Faddis Machine Tool Act

C.      For each of the questions in this section, provide:

(1)      The Public Law (or Chapter) number and Statutes at Large citation for the original legislation described.

(2)      The location of the legislation in the *U.S.C.* (Note: if it has not been codified, write "none." If it has been codified in several locations in the Code, list the citation for the earliest part of the Act codified.)

a.      What act passed by the 93rd Congress provides job training for the economically disadvantaged and under employed?

b.      What act was passed in 1954 to modify and extend the existing national defense laws?

c.      What act restored citizenship, posthumously, to Robert E. Lee in 1975.

d.      What act provides for the establishment of an American Folklife Center in the Library of Congress?

e.      What act of the 93rd Congress provides for the protection of human subjects in biomedical research?

**Drill Problem III:**

A. Using *U.S.C., U.S.C.A.,* or *U.S.C.S.,* answer the following:

1. What are the testing requirements to determine whether a substance causes cancer?

2. Where in the code is a study of the protection of whales?

3. Where in the code is the definition of "misleading advertisement"?

4. Where in the code is an employee's right to organize a labor union affirmed?

B. Using any of the popular name tables, locate the correct citation for the following (it may be necessary to consult more than one):

1. Charter School Expansion Act of 1998

2. Child Online Protection Act

3. Headstart Act of 1981

4. Sunshine Law

5. Filled Cheese Act

C. For each of the questions in this section, provide:

(1) The Public Law (or Chapter) number and Statutes at Large citation for the original legislation described.

(2) The location of the legislation in U.S.C. (Note: if it has not been codified, write "none." If it has been codified in several parts of the code, list the citation for the earliest part of the Act codified.)

a. What 1973 Act amends the Public Service Act in order to encourage the operation of health maintenance organizations?

b.      What 1972 Act authorizes the Atomic Energy Commission to issue temporary operating licenses for nuclear power plants?

c.      What 1942 joint resolution declared a state of war against the government of Hungary?

d.      What 1975 Act established the Hells Canyon National Recreation Area?

e.      What Act of the 85th Congress allowed the duty-free importation of religious regalia when it was presented free of charge to a church?

# Chapter 10

# FEDERAL LEGISLATIVE HISTORIES

**Introduction:**

The questions presented here were developed to involve the use of the five sources for legislative histories most commonly found in small to medium-sized libraries. Students should become aware of other sources such as the U.S. Library of Congress, Congressional Research Service, Digest of Public General Bills; U.S. Congress, House of Representatives, Numerical Order of Bills and Resolutions which have passed either or both Houses, and Bills now pending on the Calendar; U.S. Congress, Senate, Library, Cumulative Index of Congressional Hearings, Bill Number Index; Public Laws (slip laws). The questions were set up to include long and short questions in each section so that students may be assigned a long and a short question in each section as well as one or more of the general questions appearing at the end.

## ASSIGNMENT 1

## CONGRESSIONAL INFORMATION SERVICE

**Method:**

Use *Congressional Information Service Annuals*, 1970-75, Index volumes and tables of bill numbers, Abstract volumes and legislative histories. Answers to all questions should be cited according to rules in the latest edition of *The Bluebook* limiting citations to information found in C.I.S. Include volume, year, and pages where answers are found.

**Questions:**

1.    In 1976 legislation was enacted to extend the United States fishing limit to 200 miles to prevent foreign over-fishing off the United States coast. President Ford supported the legislation on the condition that its effective date would be delayed so that the Law of the Sea Conference could complete its work. To trace the history of the current legislation, find the following in the 1975 CIS volumes:

(a)     Senate Report of H.R. 200, 94th Congress, 1st Session. Cite report and name of committee reporting.

(b)     What CIS Abstract number would you use to find the special oversight report on H.R. 200 on microfiche?

(c)     What are the numbers of the three House bills requiring the employment of straight baselines in charting fishery zone boundaries?

2.     The Environmental Protection Agency was authorized to conduct research on the effects of noise on animals, humans and property, and one of the provisions H.R. 11,021, as cleared by Congress on October 18, 1972, made it unlawful to import excessively noisy products. You wish to read some of the testimony presented before the Senate Committee by John Tyler, head of the technical committee of the National Organization to Insure the Sound Controlled Environment, and the floor debates on the bills. Cite:

(a)     Public Law number.

(b)     Date of enactment, *Statutes at Large* and *Congressional Record* citation, Senate Hearings wherein Mr. Tyler's testimony is recorded, the Presidential Statement of October, 28, 1972.

(c)     Name of the House committee which reported on H.R. 11,021 and the House report number.

3.     Organized crime control legislation (Bomb Threat Act) was proposed in S. 30 in 1969 and 1970. You wish to read the congressional hearing of June 11, 1970, during which examples of activities of organized crime which could be prevented under the bill's provisions, such as the racketeering operations of the Mafia, the Marcello organization in New Orleans, and newspaper articles on infiltration of legitimate business by organized crime were introduced. Find:

(a)     Public Law number of the Act.

(b)     Date of enactment, *Statutes at Large* and *Congressional Record* citations. State the name of the Senate committee reporting, and the CIS Abstract number of the House hearing.

(c)     Cite House Report and Congress which recommended passage of the bill, and the name of the member of the House of Representatives from New York who stated that the bill was unconstitutional.

4.     In 1968 Congress repealed the authority which had been given to the National Science Foundation in 1958 to require persons engaging in weather modification activities to report such activities. This was repealed, and in 1971 legislation was enacted to require reporting of

weather modification activities to the Federal government. To research the need for H.R. 6893, and the possibility of future legal and international problems arising from weather modification, find the following:

(a)     Public Law number.

(b)     *Statutes at Large* and *Congressional Record* citations. CIS Abstract numbers for the House hearings.

(c)     Cite the hearings.

5.     In 1973 legislation was enacted to amend the Lead Based Paint Poisoning Act to prohibit the use of lead based paint in construction of facilities and in the manufacture of certain toys and utensils. Cite the following legislative materials in connection with S. 607:

(a)     Public Law number.

(b)     Date of enactment, *Statutes at Large* and *Congressional Record* citation, Number of 1973 Senate Report, and CIS Abstract number for microfiche.

(c)     Cite the House Conference Report which included agreements to differences concerning definitions of lead content constituting a hazard, and Congress.

6.     One of the purposes of the Deepwater Port Act of 1974 is to authorize and regulate the location, ownership, construction, and operation of deep water ports in waters beyond the territorial limits of the United States. Any adjacent coastal state directly connected by pipeline to a deep water port is affected by the Act. You are required to research further reasons for the legislation introduced in H.R. 10,701 and H.R. 11,951. Cite:

(a)     Public Law number.

(b)     Date of enactment, *Statutes at Large* citation. CIS Abstract number of the 1974 House committee print and the Presidential statement.

(c)     Cite Senate committee before which hearings were held.

(d)     Title of Senate committee print on policy issues.

7.     In December, 1971, legislation was enacted to amend the Fishermen's Protective Act of 1967 to enhance the effectiveness of international fishery conservation programs. The legislation, which had been proposed in H.R. 3304 and related bills, authorized the President to prohibit importation of fishery products from nations conducting fishery operations in a manner that diminishes effectiveness of international fishery conservation programs. Cite legislative materials in support of the above:

(a)     Public Law number.

(b)   Date of enactment, *Statutes at Large* and *Congressional Record* citations. To read the House hearings on microfiche, which CIS Abstract number would you need? Cite the House report.

(c)   The hearings also included oversight of Soviet fishing violations in the Atlantic. Where were the hearings of April 14, 1971 held, and before which House committee and subcommittee?

8.   Find a discussion of the 1973 planned cut in United States aid to the United Nations, and the extent of and need for assistance to smaller international organizations. Cite Congressional hearing and CIS Abstract number for microfiche.

9.   To support their argument that plaintiff satisfied the first requirement for determining a cause of action to be implied in 18 U.S.C. Sec. 610, the U.S. Circuit Court of Appeals, in a 1975 case, referred to the intent of the 1971 legislation which led to the Federal Election Campaign Act. To read Richard G. Kleindienst's testimony regarding political campaign spending before a Senate committee in March 1971, cite the hearing and the CIS Abstract number of the microfiche.

10.   In 1972, H.R. 9936 was enacted to provide for a current listing of each drug manufactured. What is the Public Law number? What is the name of the President of the Pharmaceutical Manufacturers' Association who testified in support of the bill? Cite the hearing.

• **ASSIGNMENT 2**

**UNITED STATES CODE CONGRESSIONAL AND ADMINISTRATIVE NEWS**

**Method:**

Use index, acts by popular names table, classification and legislative history tables, U.S. Code amendment and repeal tables, etc., in the *United States Code Congressional and Administrative News* volumes for the 88th Congress, 2nd Session through the 94th Congress, 2nd Session, to locate citations. Include Congress and session in your answers and cite in accordance with the latest edition of *The Bluebook* State volume and page where answers were located.

**Questions:**

1.      Legislation continues to be introduced in an effort to prevent the tremendous increase in juvenile crime in the hope that this is the key to controlling crime in the United States. It is said that what has been done so far has failed miserably to instill in juveniles any respect for the law through either fear or confidence. Lawyers are paid to get juveniles off just as though they were in adult criminal court and, according to recent newspaper articles, the juvenile court as it is now set up is a standing joke in the juvenile community.  Your state is in the process of rewriting its juvenile code and you have been asked to summarize the legislation which led to the Juvenile Delinquency Prevention and Control act of 1968. Cite the following:

    (a)     Public Law number and *Statutes at Large* citation.
    (b)     U.S. Code citation.
    (c)     Date of approval, House bill number, full  names of House and Senate committees  reporting, and *Congressional Record* citation.
    (d)     Who did Mr. Javits quote in connection with this legislation?

2.      On July 6, 1976, President Ford signed S. 2853 (Pub. L. No. 94- 339) to tighten up the accountability of food stamp vendors. On signing the bill, the President expressed disappointment that it was not a major revision of the program and stated that each day that goes by without congressional action to reform the food stamp program costs taxpayers about three million dollars. You have some questions about the integrity of the program. To research the legislation which led to the 1964 Act, cite the following:

    (a)     Public Law number of the 1964 Act and the *Statutes at Large* citation.

    (b)    House bill number, Congress and session, Congressional Record citation. Date House considered passage of the bill, and the name of the committee reporting.

    (c)    Find the analysis of the House bill and cite the number of the section dealing with the redemption of coupons.

3.    Major legislation was enacted in 1976 to revitalized the nation's railroads, and a new government agency was created to take over the operations of some of the bankrupt Northeast and Midwest railroads. You wish to research the background of the legislation which was enacted in 1973 to salvage the rail services operated by seven insolvent railroads in the same regions. Cite:

    (a)    Public Law number of the 1973 Act and the *Statutes at Large* citation.

    (b)    United States Code titles which were affected.

    (c)    Date of approval, House bill number, Committee and Congress, *Congressional Record* citation.

    (d)    The names of the four members who stated that, in their view, this legislation wrote into law a detailed collective bargaining agreement negotiated between railway management and labor, and paid for out of the Federal treasury.

4.    On July 22, 1975, Attorney General Edward H. Levi presented to the Senate Judiciary Subcommittee on Juvenile Delinquency the Ford Administration's proposed gun control bill, which was intended to correct the flaws in the 1968 Gun Control Act. By September, 1975, the House Judiciary Subcommittee on Crime had 127 bills pending before it and both committees had held extensive hearings on gun control. To research the "flaws" in the 1968 Act find and cite the following:

    (a)    Public Law number and *Statutes at Large* citation.

    (b)    United States Code classification for Title I, Secs. 101-105 of the Act.

    (c)    The Senate Report, the name of the committee reporting and the *Congressional Record* citation.

    (d)    In Conference Report No. 1956 the title proposed for the Act by the Senate was adopted in lieu of that proposed by the House. Cite the title provided in the House bill.

5.    A 1965 study entitled "The Older Worker - Age Discrimination in Employment" was reported by the Secretary of Labor. In 1967 legislation was introduced to correct this, and during Congressional hearings concerning the age limitation witnesses representing airline stewardesses

revealed an apparent gross and arbitrary employment distinction based on age alone. To read the history of the 1967 Act cite the following:

(a)     Public Law number and *Statutes at Large* citation.

(b)     United States Code classification.

(c)     Bill number, Congress House committee reporting and *Congressional Record* citation.

(d)     How many states were cited as having age discrimination legislation of the type proposed in the House bill?

6.      The coastal zone management concept which involved some time in the mid-1960s led to the passage of federal legislation in 1972. Under the Act, and subsequent amendments, after a state has adopted a program and has it federally approved, federal actions are to be consistent with that state's program, giving the state additional leverage over federal agency actions. There is a developing legal area that is a major concern of the states, and you wish to evaluate the key issues and incentives in the coastal management program. Cite the following:

(a)     Public Law number of the 1972 Act, *Statutes at Large* citation.

(b)     United States Code classification.

(c)     Date of approval of the Act. Senate bill number, Congress, and name of Senate Committee reporting, date of passage, and *Congressional Record* citation.

(d)     In his letter to Mr. Magnuson dated April 20, 1970, Mr. Robert R. Keller, Assistant Comptroller General of the United States, suggested a change in the bill regarding the acquisition of real property. What change did he suggest?

7.      In his October 1973 anti-inflation message to Congress, President Ford requested new penalties for persons and corporations violating the antitrust laws. A bill to amend the antitrust laws with regard to the conduct of consent decree procedures resulted in legislation in 1974. Cite the following:

(a)     Public Law number and *Statutes at Large* citation.

(b)     The titles of the United States Code affected.

(c)     The number of the bill introducing the legislation and Congress. Date the House passed the bill and the name of the committee reporting, and *Congressional Record* citation.

(d)     Having found a discussion of the legislation, state name of the person who introduced the first of the three bills relating to Antitrust Procedures and Penalties.

8.      Cite the proper title of the 1975 Hazardous Materials Transportation Act, amendment, and Public Law number.

9.   Cite the popular title of the provisions enacted under Public Law No. 93-638.

10   Give the Public Law number and the *Statutes at Large* citation of the legislation which was  enacted as a result of H.R. 19,436 in 1970.

## ASSIGNMENT 3

### DRILL PROBLEMS

**Drill Problem I:**

A.      Using the array of research tools introduced in the chapter, answer the following. Provide full citations where appropriate.

1.      What is the number of the Senate Report on Pub. L. No. 94-427, the Olympic Games Authorization Act of 1976?

2.      On June 21, 1977, John J. Duncan made seven pages of testimony to a House subcommittee:
(a)      What bill did the testimony concern?
(b)      What is the CIS fiche code number?
(c)      What is its Superintendent of Documents number?

3.      On what date did the Senate consider and pass Pub. L No. 94-34?

4.      What is the *Statutes at Large* citation for Pub. L. No. 95-209?

5.      What does the abbreviation C.P.I. stand for?

B.      Using the Index and Daily Digest volumes of the *Congressional Record,* answer the following for the First Session of the 93rd Congress:

(a)      Give the number of two Senate Reports on S-9.
(b)      What was the subject of S. 2534?
(c)      What legislation was passed in lieu of H.R. 9682?
(d)      What was the number of the bill that was enacted as Pub. L. No. 93-222?
(e)      What bills were introduced in the Senate on Monday, May 21, 1973?

C.      Use the *U.S. Code Congressional and Administrative News* volumes to answer the following:

1.      Using the 1978 *U.S.C.C.A.N.,* answer the following:
(a)      What are the Committee assignments of Congressperson Jack Brinkley?

(b)     Why is there no excerpt printed of the Senate Report on the Presidential Records Act of 1978?

2.     Using the 1972 *U.S.C.C.A.N.,* answer the following:
   (a)     What were the Committee assignments of Delbert Latta?
   (b)     What documents are printed as part of the legislative history of the Equal Employment Opportunity Act of 1972?

3.     Using the 1974 *U.S.C.C.A.N.,* answer the following:
   (a)     What is the *Statutes at Large* citation for Pub. L. No. 93-558?
   (b)     What reports were made on the Egg Research bill?

**Drill Problem II:**

A.     Using the array of research tools introduced in the chapter, answer the following. Provide full citations where appropriate.

1.     On what date did the President make a statement concerning Pub. L. No. 94-158?

2.     On May 17, 1973, Rowland F. Kirks made a statement, and participated in a discussion during hearings on S. 1533.
   (a)     What Committee and Subcommittee sponsored the hearings?
   (b)     What document was discussed by Mr. Kirks during the hearings?

3.     What was the number of the bill that became Pub. L. No. 94-68?

4.     On what topic did Professor Shepard Forman testify on June 28, 1977?

5.     Find a discussion of the 1974 planned cut in United States aid to the United Nations and the extent of the need for assistance to smaller international organizations. Cite the congressional hearing and CIS Abstract number for the microfiche.

B.     Using the Index and Daily Digest volumes of the *Congressional Record* answer the following:

1.     For the First Session of the 91st Congress:

(a)     What bill was the basis of Pub. L. No. 91-54?

(b)     What was the topic of H.R. 12,542?

(c)     What was the final disposition of H.R. 7206?

(d)     On what two subjects did the President submit messages to the Senate on August 6, 1969?

(e)     To what committee was H.R. 9198 referred?

(f)     What was the topic of Senate Joint Resolution 18?

C.     Use the *U.S. Code Congressional and Administrative News* volumes to answer the following:

1.     Using the 1978 *U.S.C.C.A.N.,* answer the following:
   (a)     Who is the Chairman of the House Standing Committee on Interstate and Foreign Commerce?
   (b)     List the reports that accompanied the Amateur Sports Act of 1978.

2.     Using the 1972 *U.S.C.C.A.N.,* answer the following:
   (a)     What was the subject of Presidential Proclamation No. 4169?
   (b)     What is the number of the House Conference Report on the Coastal Zone Management Act of 1972?

3.     Using the 1974 *U.S.C.C.A.N.,* answer the following:
   (a)     What is the subject of Presidential Proclamation No. 4331?
   (b)     Who was the chairman of the Senate Foreign Relations Committee?

**Drill Problem III:**

A.     Using the array of research tools introduced in the chapter, answer the following. Provide full citations where appropriate.

1.     What is the CIS code number for the House Veteran's Affairs Committee?

2.     What is the CIS fiche code number for S. Rept. 93-338?

3.     What House and Senate committees reported on Pub. L. No. 95-100?

4.      What is the CIS fiche number for the Senate Report on Pub. L. No. 95-25?

5.      Cite the Public Law number and title of the legislation enacted at the end of 1974, which removed social service programs from heir prior close connection with cash public assistance programs, and set up a separate title in the Social Security Act. Where can you read he Presidential statement in connection with his legislation?

B.      Using the Index and Daily Digest volumes of the *Congressional Record,* answer the following.

1.      For the First Session of the 92d Congress:
        (a)     Give the Senate report number on S.557.
        (b)     What was the subject of H.R. 237?
        (c)     How many private bills were enacted into law by this session of Congress?
        (d)     What was the number of the bill that was enacted into Pub. L. No. 92-92?
        (e)     To which committee was H.R. 248 referred?
        (f)     On which page of the *Congressional Record* would you find an article about "Hoosier Hippies"?

C.      Use the *U.S. Code Congressional and Administrative News* volumes to answer the following.

1.      Using the 1978 *U.S.C.C.A.N.,* answer the following:
        (a)     Excerpts of what reports are printed as legislative history for Pub. L. No. 95- 375?
        (b)     On what date did the House finally pass on the Consumer Co-operative Bank Act?

2.      Using the 1972 *U.S.C.C.A.N.,* answer the following:
        (a)     What is the number of the House Conference Committee report on the Pesticide Control Act? Is it included in *U.S.C.C.A.N.?*
        (b)     What documents are published in *U.S.C.C.A.N.* as legislative history for the Volunteers in the National Forest Act of 1972?

3.      Using the 1974 U.S.C.C.A.N., answer the following:

(a)     What documents are printed in *U.S.C.C.A.N.* to accompany the Education Amendments of 1974?

(b)     What reports on Pub. L. No. 93-383 are not published in *U.S.C.C.A.N.?*

# Chapter 11

# STATE AND MUNICIPAL LEGISLATION

## ASSIGNMENT 1

### STATE LEGISLATION -- GENERAL

**Method:**

Answer all questions of this assignment using legislative sources for your own state. Cite in accord with the latest edition of *The Bluebook*. Cite either specific or illustrative authority as appropriate. Because the questions found in this assignment are cumulative, rather than repetitive, the student should answer each for his/her own jurisdiction.

**Questions:**

Note: Answers to each question will vary according to state.

1. Identify the statutory compilation(s) within your jurisdiction.

2. What is the authoritative force of the compilation(s)?

3. Describe the method(s) of supplementation of the compilation(s).

4. Is there a general index to the compilation(s)? Are there separate indexes for individual volumes or titles?

5. What is the most significant difference between the scope of coverage of the general and the separate indexes?

6. Is the index to the compilation(s) arranged topically and factually? Or only topically?

7. Are the references in the general index to compilation sections or to page numbers?

8.    In your jurisdiction is there an overall index to general, special, local and temporary acts which are not included in the statutory compilation(s)?

9.    How, if at all, are cases construing provisions of the compilation(s) located?

10.   Does the compilation(s) include references or citations to opinions of the state attorney general? If so, where are they found?

11.   Indicate the cross references, if any, to other non-statutory research aids found in the compilation(s).

12.   Does the compilation(s) contain textual commentaries or general historical essays?

13.   Describe the historical notes, if any, given for each section of the compilation(s).

14.   Are there cross references to related sections of the compilation(s)? Where are they found?

15.   Are cross references to comparable legislation in other jurisdictions given in the compilation(s)? If not, locate a compilation containing such cross references.

16.   Is the effective date of each section of the compilation(s) given? If not, what date is given? Where would one find the effective date?

17.   Is there a separate table of acts by popular names? If not how are acts by popular names indexed?

18.   Are there parallel references from earlier compilations to the present? Where are they located? If not, how does one trace from a prior compilation to a current compilation?

19.   Is there a reference table from the session laws of the state to the compilation(s)? Where is the table located?

20.   Does the index to your state constitution contain specific terms leading you directly to cases construing the constitution?

21.     Describe the general procedure to be followed in locating specific cases construing a provision of your state constitution.

22.     Locate and cite the "due process" clause of your state constitution.

23.     Under the constitution of your state, can a minor traffic violation be used as justification to search the car of a defendant without a search warrant?

24.     Does your state compilation(s) include the United States Constitution? If yes, is it annotated? Where is it located?

25.     Does your state have a formalized procedure for advising one of pending legislation? If so, describe it.

## ASSIGNMENT 2

## STATE CODES--USE OF INDEXES

**Method:**

Using the index to the latest code of your state, locate the current statutory laws on the following subjects:

**Questions:**

1.    Arbitration laws.

2.    Pollution laws.

3.    Powers of attorney laws.

4.    Landlord and tenant laws.

5.    Specific performance laws.

6.    Chiropractors laws.

7.    Fictitious name laws.

8.    Franchise laws.

9.    Gambling laws.

10.   Gifts to minors laws.

11.   Descent and distribution laws.

12.   Extradition laws.

13.   Fraud laws.

14.   Hunting laws.

15.   Insolvency laws.

16.   Municipal corporations laws.

17.   Drug laws.

18.   Mechanics' liens laws.

19.   Trademarks and tradenames laws.

20. Trust companies laws.

21. Attachment laws.

22. Housing laws.

23. Workmen's compensation laws.

24. Birth certificates laws.

25. Nursing homes laws.

26. Capital punishment, existence of.

27. Next of kin, who is?

28. Homicide, definition of.

29. Homestead exemptions.

30. Legislation governing use of state flag.

# ASSIGNMENT 3

## STATE CODES -- CONSTRUCTION

**Method:**

Using bound volumes, bound supplements, specific pamphlet supplements, pocket parts, general pamphlet supplements, the tables of statutes construed from the appropriate reporter bound volumes and advance sheets, cite the *most recent* case construing each statute in Assignment 2.

**Questions:**

QUESTIONS: Numbers 1 - 30 from Assignment 2.

# ASSIGNMENT 4

## STATE CODES -- DERIVATION

**Method:**

Using the same sources employed in Assignment 2, locate and cite the oldest legislation noted as part of the history of each of the statutes found as a result thereof. Cite in accord with the latest edition of *The Bluebook.*

**Questions:**

Numbers 1 - 30 from Assignment 2.

## ASSIGNMENT 5

## STATE SESSION LAWS -- PARALLEL REFERENCE TABLES

**Method:**

Using parallel reference tables from the appropriate state codes, convert the following citations to their current equivalent.

**Questions:**

1.  1935 Del. Code sec. 575.

2.  1863 Ga. Code sec. 3796.

3.  1955 Hawaii Rev. Laws sec. 30-9.

4.  1919 Ida. Comp. Stat. sec. 3201.

5.  1924 Iowa Code, sec. 5147.

6.  1954 Maine Rev. Stat. c. 144, sec. 7.

7.  1930 Miss. Code sec. 4941.

8.  1942 N.H. Rev. Laws sec. 229:71.

9.  1929 N. Mex. Comp. Stat. sec. 4-2103.

10. 1910 Okla. Rev. Laws sec. 7381.

# ASSIGNMENT 6

## STATE CODES -- COMPARATIVE RESEARCH

**Sources:**    *Model Business Corporation Act Annotated* (4<sup>th</sup> ed. 2008).
*Martindale-Hubbell Law Directory* (latest).
*Book of the States*(latest).

## Method:

Using the sources listed above, answer the following questions. When required, cite sources in accord with the latest edition *The Bluebook.*

## Questions:

A       Use the *Model Business Corporation Act Annotated,* 4<sup>th</sup> ed.

   1.      Locate and cite the section on voluntary dissolution by act of the corporation. Is this model act provision identical or comparable with that of your state? If so, cite your state's statute.

   2.      Locate and cite the appropriate section on failure of the corporation to hold annual meetings. Does any state have a provision identical in substance with this section? If so, cite that state's statute.

   3.      Locate the section dealing with payment of cash dividends; indicate whether the Model Act provision is identical with that of your state.

   4.      What is the minimum number of directors required for a corporation? What do the corporation laws of your home state and the states contiguous thereto require?

B.      Use *Martindale-Hubbell Law Directory* (latest). For each answer, give the subject heading(s) under which the answer was found, the jurisdictions, and the authority specified in Martindale-Hubbell. Give answers for Alabama, Louisiana and Mississippi.

   1.      Age of majority.

2. Time specified by statute of limitations to recover damages for wrongful death.

3. Drug use as a ground for divorce.

4. Seat of the supreme court, i.e., highest court of appeal.

C. Use *Book of the States* (latest). For all answers, give the page on which the answers were found.

1. Identify the states having the highest and lowest individual income tax rates. Specify the rates.

2. What is the method of selecting Supreme Court Justices in Alabama, Louisiana, and Mississippi?

3. How long does it take for a bill in Iowa to become law unless vetoed by the governor during the session?

# ASSIGNMENT 7

## MARTINDALE-HUBBELL LAW DIRECTORY FOREIGN LAW DIGESTS

**Method:**

Using the summaries of foreign legislation in the Law Digests volume of the *Martindale-Hubbell Law Directory*, ascertain whether alcoholism or drunkenness constitute grounds for either a divorce or a separation in the following countries:

1. Argentina

2. Australia

3. Columbia

4. Costa Rica

5. Chile

6. Guatemala causes domestic discord.

7. Ireland (Eire)

8. Italy

9. Mexico

10. Venezuela

## ASSIGNMENT 8

## DRILL PROBLEMS

**Drill Problem I:**

Locate the following:

1.  The code section designating the Cherokee rose Georgia's State Floral Emblem.

2.  The Hawaii Code section about a special fund for the cost to quarantine animals.

3.  The current state code cites for the following:

    (a)  1965 Ill. Laws p.3698 § 1.
    (b)  1935 Ind. Acts Ch. 128 § 1.
    (c)  1927 Iowa Code § 13615.
    (d)  Ky. Carroll's Civ. Code § 460.

**Drill Problem II:**

Locate the following:

1.  The section of the Maryland code requiring the clerks of county courts to endorse each deed to real property.

2.  The section of the Massachusetts code providing minimum wage for golf caddies.

3.  The current state code cites for the following:

    (a)  1969 Minn. Laws Ch. 895 §1.
    (b)  1972 Mo. Laws, p. 605 § 1.
    (c)  1942 Miss. Code § 1186.
    (d)  1979 N.H. Laws Ch. 492 § 1.

# Chapter 12

# COURT RULES AND PROCEDURES

## ASSIGNMENT 1

### FEDERAL RULES OF CIVIL PROCEDURE

**Sources:**    Title 28 *United States Code Annotated* or *United States Code Service* covering 1-86 of the *Federal Rules of Civil Procedure.*

C. Wright & A. Miller, *Federal Practice and Procedure* covering *Federal Rules of Civil Procedure.*

J. Moore, *Moore's Federal Practice* (3d ed.) covering *Federal Rules of Civil Procedure.*

**Method:**

Briefly answer the questions. Cite to rule numbers, treatises and cases as required. Use any of the sources listed above.

**Questions and Answers:**

1.  QUESTION:    Cite the section in *Moore* that discusses the Supreme Court's authority to promulgate rules of procedure under the Rule-Making Statute of 1934.

2.  QUESTION:    In what years have subdivisions (b), (d)(4), (d)(7), (e), and (f) of Rule 4 been changed?

3.  QUESTION:    What rule prescribes a uniform method of service upon the United States in all actions governed by the Federal Rules?

4.  QUESTION:    Cite the rule which indicates if it is a requirement that the signing of pleadings must always be verified or accompanied by an affidavit.

5.    QUESTION:        In what year was Rule 6(c) rescinded?
                       Why was this rule rendered unnecessary?

6.    QUESTION:        Cite the rule regarding depositions pending
                       appeal.

7.    QUESTION:        Using *Wright & Miller,* cite a 1958 6th
                       Circuit case in which a bank sought a
                       declaratory judgment that it would be
                       unlawful for a state bank to open a branch
                       in the same city. Cite also the section in
                       *Wright & Miller* under which the case is
                       cited.

8.    QUESTION:        If a court orders separate trials as provided
                       in rule 42(b), judgment on a counterclaim
                       or cross-claim may be rendered in
                       accordance with what rule?

9.    QUESTION:        Rule 14 was modeled on what Admiralty
                       Rule?

10.   QUESTION:        Rule 23(a) is a substantial restatement of
                       what earlier Equity Rule?

11.   QUESTION:        Under the Federal Rules, does the court
                       have the power to order a summary
                       judgment without a hearing? Cite
                       applicable rules and section in *Wright &
                       Miller.*

12.   QUESTION:        Is shareholder-plaintiff in a successful
                       derivative action entitled to reimbursement
                       of attorney's fees? Cite applicable section
                       in *Wright & Miller.*

13.   QUESTION:        Upon motion, the court may order that
                       testimony taken at disposition be recorded
                       by other than stenographic means. If so,
                       should the order designate the manner of
                       recording? Cite rule number.

# ASSIGNMENT 2

## FEDERAL RULES OF CRIMINAL PROCEDURE

**Sources:** Title 18 *United States Code Annotated* or *United States Code Service* covering Rules 1-60 of the *Federal Rules of Criminal Procedure*

C. Wright and A. Miller, *Federal Practice and Procedure* covering the *Federal Rules of Criminal Procedure.*

J. Moore, *Moore's Federal Practice* (3d ed.) covering the *Federal Rules of Criminal Procedure.*

## Method:

Briefly answer the questions. Cite to rule numbers, treatises and cases as required. Use any of the sources listed above.

## Questions and Answers:

1.  QUESTION:    When used in the *Federal Rules of Criminal Procedure,* does the word "state" include the District of Columbia? Cite applicable rule.

2.  QUESTION:    May a defendant waive his right to preliminary examination? Cite applicable rule.

3.  QUESTION:    Is it proper for an attorney for the government to challenge a grand juror after the oath to the grand juror has been administered? Cite pertinent rule.

4.  QUESTION:    Must a motion raising defenses and objections based on defects in the institution of the prosecution always be made before trial? Cite pertinent rule.

5.  QUESTION:    Are statements made by accused in psychiatric examination admissible as

evidence against the accused on the issue of guilt? Cite rule.

6.  QUESTION: According to *United States v. FLores,* is the record of prior criminal convictions of persons whom government intends to call as witnesses at trial discovered under Rule 16.

7.  QUESTION: Rule 17(f) of the *Federal Rules of Criminal Procedure* is substantially the same as what rule of the *Federal Rules of Civil* Procedure?

8.  QUESTION: Cite a rule which indicates if the indigent defendant in a criminal case has the right to secure attendance of witnesses at the expense to the Government.

9.  QUESTION: When did the rule establishing a basis for pretrial conferences with counsel for the parties in criminal cases become effective? Cite pertinent rule.

10. QUESTION: Under what circumstances may a jury consist of less than twelve persons? Cite pertinent rule.

11. QUESTION: If a judge presiding over a case dies prior to sentencing, must the successor judge always order a new trial? Cite pertinent rule.

12. QUESTION: A motion for a new trial based on grounds other than newly discovered evidence must normally be made within how many days of a verdict? Cite pertinent rule.

13. QUESTION: What rule gives a court discretion in deciding whether to stay an order placing a defendant on probation?

14. QUESTION: Who may request that a search warrant be issued? Cite pertinent rule.

15.  QUESTION:  If a judge certifies that he actually saw or heard conduct constituting contempt being committed in the actual presence of the court, is it necessary for the contempt to be prosecuted on notice? Cite pertinent rules.

# ASSIGNMENT 3

## USE OF FEDERAL PROCEDURE FORMS

**Sources:**     *West's Federal Forms*

*Federal Procedural Forms* (Lawyers' Edition)

## Method:

Using the source indicated, locate forms, citing volume number, page number, and section number, when applicable.

## Questions and Answers:

A.     Use *West's Federal Forms:*

1.     QUESTION:     An order granting motion for summary judgment and dismissing motion for preliminary injunction.

2.     QUESTION:     Claim of owner to articles seized under Food and Drug Act.

3.     QUESTION:     Order for writ of habeas corpus.

4.     QUESTION:     A pre-trial order in a railroad crossing accident case.

5.     QUESTION:     A jury instruction on creditability of a child witness.

B.     Use *Federal Procedural Forms* (Lawyers Edition):

1.     QUESTION:     Form for attorney affidavit in support of a motion for new trial.

2.     QUESTION:     Complaint for common law trademark infringement for use of plaintiff's corporate name.

3.      QUESTION:              Motion for new trial in action tried by jury.

4.      QUESTION:              Order for discharge of a trustee in
                              bankruptcy.

5.      QUESTION:              Motion in Supreme Court to dismiss an
                              appeal for lack of jurisdiction.

# ASSIGNMENT 4

## COURT RULES

**Method:**

Use the court rules volumes of *United State Code Annotated* (U.S.C.A.) and/or *United States Code Service* (U.S.C.S.) to answer the following questions, citing the rule number:

**Questions and Answers:**

1. QUESTION: Under the *Federal Rules of Appellate Procedure,* is leave or consent required for a state to file an amicus curiae brief?

2. QUESTION: Unless the Court has provided otherwise, at what time is the appendix to a brief to be filed in a United States Court of Appeals?

3. QUESTION: May anyone remove books from the Supreme Court Library?

4. QUESTION: In the Supreme Court, how much time is usually allowed for oral argument?

5. QUESTION: Before the Supreme Court will admit an attorney applying to practice in the Court, she/he must have been admitted to practice in the highest court of a state, etc., for how long?

6. QUESTION: What rule provides for law students to appear in the United States Court of Appeals for the District of Columbia?

# ASSIGNMENT 5

# WRIGHT & MILLER, FEDERAL PRACTICE AND PROCEDURE

## Method:

Using C. Wright & A. Miller, *Federal Practice and Procedure,* answer the following questions, giving citations where necessary.

## Questions and Answers:

1. QUESTION: What 1952 Supreme Court case upheld the admissibility of evidence obtained through use of a "wired" undercover agent in a criminal case?

2. QUESTION: Where is there discussion of the meaning of the word "admissible" as used in Rule 402 of the *Federal Rules of* Evidence?

3. QUESTION: Where are the implications of "negative pregnants" in the *Federal Rules of Civil Procedure* discussed?

4. QUESTION: Where can one find the forms mentioned in Rule 84 of *Federal Rules of Civil* Procedure?

5. QUESTION: Which of the *Federal Rules of Criminal Procedure* gave government a right to discovery against criminal defendants for the first time?

6. QUESTION: Where is there discussion of pretrial conferences in complex cases?

7. QUESTION: May an injunction be binding on unnamed members of a labor union?

8. QUESTION: Where is there a discussion of the law controlling the question of immunity from service of process?

# Chapter 13

# ADMINISTRATIVE LAW

## ASSIGNMENT

## USE OF THE CODE OF FEDERAL REGULATIONS

**Sources:**          *C.F.R. Index and Finding Aids*

**Method:**

Using any of the available indexes to the C.F.R., locate and cite the appropriate title and section for each of the following problems:

**Note to Instructors:**          Pathfinders are to *C.F.R. Index.* Other sources will have different index terms and page numbers.

**Questions:**

1.      Where in the C.F.R. is it specifically stated that it is an unlawful employment practice to classify a job as "male" or "female" or to maintain separate lines of progression or separate seniority lists based on sex where this would adversely affect any employee unless sex is a bona fide occupational qualification for the job?

2.      In which C.F.R. title and section does the Occupational Safety and Health Administration of the Department of Labor specify the amount of airborne concentrations of asbestos fibers to which an employee may be exposed in an eight hour period?

3.      Under which C.F.R. title and part is the procedure for reporting natural gas pipeline leaks given?

4.      What C.F.R. title and section governs the withholding of U.S. Government checks which are intended for delivery in certain countries where it has been determined that postal, transportation,

or banking facilities are such that there is not a reasonable assurance that named payees in those areas will actually receive these checks and be able to negotiate them for full value?

5.    Where in the C.F.R. is the provision establishing a maximum liability of fifty dollars per card for credit card holders in cases involving unauthorized use of such cards?

6.    Where in the C.F.R. is it specified that misuse of the word "perfect" in describing a diamond is an unfair trade practice?

7.    Where in the C.F.R. is the description of the signaling arrangements, i.e., the attention signal, whereby standard, FM, and television broadcast stations can actuate muted receivers for the receipt of cueing announcements as part of the Emergency Broadcast System?

8.    Where in the C.F.R. are the provisions which deal with the "Warnings" which packages of antacid products for human use must carry to avoid being misbranded?

9.    Where in the C.F.R. are the reporting requirements for accidents involving the transportation of radioactive materials?

10.    The Postal regulations provide that the Domestic Mail Manual is available for reference and inspection at various places including all U.S. Post Offices and branches. What portion thereof deals with Postage Meters and Meter Stamps?

11.    Where in the C.F.R. is the provision governing the use of non-federal funds in federally sponsored vocational rehabilitation programs for the mentally retarded?

12.    Where in the C.F.R. are the federal grade standards for frozen okra enumerated?

13.    Where in the C.F.R. are the provisions as authorized by the Federal Truth in Lending Act which govern the determination of finance charges?

14.    Where in the C.F.R. are the provisions covering the labeling requirements for "Lemon Juice?"

15. Where in the C.F.R. are the provisions governing the service of process and subpoenas upon personnel of the Department of the Navy?

16. Where in the Domestic Mail Manual are the provisions governing commemorative stamps?

17. What section of the Postal Service title discusses plant protection and quarantining importation of plants and plant products by mail?

18. Where in the C.F.R. are the provisions of the Social Security Administration covering insurance benefits for victims of black lung disease?

19. Where in the C.F.R. are the provisions of the Food and Drug Administration specifying the standard of fill for a container of canned applesauce?

20. Where in the C.F.R. are there provisions dealing with the rate of import tax on beer as of the time of its importation, or, if entered into customs custody, at the time of removal from such custody?

21. 42 U.S.C. §263 is the federal law authorizing the U.S. Public Health Service to prepare certain biological products when not available from licensed establishments. Cite C.F.R. parts issued under this statute as shown in the *C.F.R. Index and Finding Aids*.

22. Pollution of navigable waters by the discharge of oil of all types is covered by what title and part of the C.F.R.?

23. Locate the C.F.R. definition of "cable television service."

24. Where can you find the regulations dealing with the Marine Mammal Protection Act of 1972?

25. Federal flood insurance regulations define the coverage of this insurance. Are mud slides covered? Cite the definition regulation for this.

26. Any person may bring to the attention of the Civil Rights Commission a grievance believed to fall within its jurisdiction. Should the complaint include the names and titles of the officials

or other persons involved in acts forming the basis for the complaint?

27. There are quarantine regulations which the U.S. Surgeon General administers. Cite the regulation which lists the various diseases that are "Quarantinable."

28. Are consular or other foreign service officers permitted to celebrate marriages? What regulation covers the consular office acting as an official witness to a marriage?

29. Where can you find how a contract is awarded for harvesting timber on public land?

30. Are Native American graves protected on public land?

# Chapter 14

# LOOSELEAF SERVICES

## ASSIGNMENT 1

## USE OF LOOSELEAF SERVICES OR REPORTERS

**Method:**

Briefly answer the question and give the citation requested using the form required by the latest edition of *The Bluebook* to the extent that the indicated source provides the information needed for such a citation.

**Questions:**

1.  Source: C.C.H. *Standard Federal Tax Reporter.* Where a taxpayer does not establish a basis for measuring an alleged casualty loss of ornamental trees, will a deduction be allowed? Cite the C.C.H. paragraph on point.

2.  Source: C.C.H. *Standard Federal Tax Reporter.* Was a newspaper subscriber taxable on the value of an automobile which he won on a lottery ticket received with his subscription as part of a campaign by the newspaper to increase its circulation? Cite a case on point.

3.  Source: C.C.H. *Standard Federal Tax Reporter.* May a member of the U.S. foreign service, i.e., a consular officer, take a business traveling expense deduction for transportation, meals, and lodging that is occasioned by being on "home leave?" Cite a Revenue Ruling on point.

4.  Source: C.C.H. *Standard Federal Tax* Reporter. May letter carriers deduct the cost and maintenance expenses of uniforms? Cite a Revenue Ruling on point.

5.  Source: C.C.H. *Standard Federal Tax Reporter.* Is the amount of a dissolved partnership debt paid by a former partner on behalf of a deceased partner's insolvent estate deductible? Cite a Revenue Ruling on point.

6.      Source: C.C.H. *Standard Federal Tax Reporter.* In some cases may the cost of improvements made by business tenants in lieu of paying rent be deductible as rent? Cite the C.C.H. paragraph on point.

7.      Source: C.C.H. *Standard Federal Tax Reporter.* Are travel expenses of teachers on sabbatical leave deductible if and to the extent that the travel is directly related to the duties of the teacher in his teaching position? Cite a Revenue Ruling on point.

8.      Source: C.C.H. *Standard Federal Tax Reporter.* Were the legal fees incurred in an unsuccessful attempt to have a liquor license transferred from one bar to another building which the taxpayer owned deductible? Cite a case on point.

9.      Source: C.C.H. *Standard Federal Tax Reporter.* Is a monthly charge or "tax" made by a city for the use of its sewer system a deductible personal expense as are property taxes? Cite the C.C.H. paragraph on point.

10.     Source: C.C.H. *Standard Federal Tax Reporter.* Are legal expenses deductible where incurred by a husband in resisting his wife's suit for divorce? Cite the U.S. Sup. Ct. cases on point.

11.     Source: C.C.H. *Standard Federal Tax Reporter.* Does the operation of a dining room, cafeteria, and snack bar by an exempt art museum for the use of its employees and members of the visiting public constitute an unrelated business activity? Cite the pertinent Revenue Ruling so determining.

12.     Source: C.C.H. *Standard Federal Tax Reporter.* A stock purchase plan for an employee allowed him to buy stock with a current market value of $100 by paying only $85 per share for it. Will he be taxable on the $15 difference in value at the time he purchases this stock? What section of the Int. Rev. Code applies here?

## ASSIGNMENT 2

## USE OF LOOSELEAF SERVICE CITATORS

**Method:**

Answer the question by giving the citator reference as shown or otherwise providing the information requested.

**Questions:**

1. Source: C.C.H. *Standard Federal Tax Reporter Citator.* The *Las Vegas Land Water Co.* case. 26 T.C. 881. was cited in a later opinion of the Tax Court. What is the *Tax Court Reports* citation for the citing case?

2. Source: C.C.H. *Standard Federal Tax Reporter Citator.* The case of *Phillips v. Howe Films Co.* was first decided by a Federal District Court for Pennsylvania. Was this decision affirmed or reversed by the Third Circuit?

3. Source: C.C.H. *Federal Estate and Gift Tax Reporter*, vol. 3. You are looking for the case involving the *Estate of Frank Janson.* What part of the official citation can be developed from the citator?

4. Source: C.C.H. *Standard Federal Tax Reporter Citator.* Which federal courts heard the case of *Rose E. Roybark*?

5. Source: C.C.H. *Standard Federal Tax Reporter Citator.* Did the Commissioner of Internal Revenue indicate acquiesce in the holding of the Tax Court in the case involving *Lola G. Bullard,* 5 T.C. 1346? In what volume of the *Cumulative Bulletin* is the Commissioner's action reported?

6. Source: C.C.H. *Standard Federal Tax Reporter Citator.* The United States Court of Appeals affirmed the Tax Court in the case involving *William E. Conroy.* Did the action of the Court of Appeals appear in a full opinion or a per curiam opinion?

7. Source: C.C.H. *Federal Estate and Gifts Tax Reporter,* vol. 3. The case of *Leonard D. Reeves, Admr. (Est. of T.K. Reeves) v. U.S.,* 57 U.S.T.C. para. 11,717, was cited in what 1971 Revenue Ruling?

8.	Source: C.C.H. *Standard Federal Tax Reporter Citator.* Did the U.S. court of Appeals for the Sixth Circuit reverse or affirm the Tax Court in the case involving George L. Sogg?

9.	Source: C.C.H. *Standard Federal Tax Reporter Citator.* Who appealed the decision of the United States Board of Tax Appeals to the U.S. Court of Appeals in the case involving *Little Gem Coal* Company?

10.	Source: C.C.H. *Federal Estate and Gifts Tax Reporter Citator.* What is the citation for the *Snyder* case which cited *Worcester County Trust Co. (Est. of E.E. Aldrich) v.* U.S.?

11.	Source: *Pike and Fischer Radio Regulation Finding Aids Volume.* Give the first citation of 27 F.C.C.2d 743 that appears in 71 R.R.2d.

12.	Source: *Pike and Fischer Radio Regulation Finding Aids Volume.* The Fairness Doctrine Rules appeared in 10 R.R.2d 1901. Find the last citation to these rules that appears in 24 R.R.2d.

13.	Source: C.C.H. *Standard Federal Tax Reporter Citator.* Did the Commissioner acquiesce in the Tax Court decision involving *John F. Lewis,* Jr.? Give as shown the action of the Third Circuit Court of Appeals in this case.

14.	Source: C.C.H. *Standard Federal Tax Reporter Citator.* The Court of Appeals decision of *Mrs. Leonie G. Mayer v. Donnelly* was cited in a later decision, the *Swenson* case. What is the citation of such *Swenson* decision?

15.	Source: C.C.H. *Standard Federal Tax Reporter Citator.* Did the U.S. Supreme Court grant certiorari in the *Francis Doll* case? The Eighth Circuit *Doll* opinion was cited in *Northwest Security National Bank.* Give the citator reference to this latter decision as shown.

16.	Source: C.C.H. *Standard Federal Tax Reporter* at Case Table. Was the District Court decision in *Ralph M. Currie, Jr. v. Internal Revenue Service* affirmed *by* the Court of Appeals for the 11th Circuit? Give the U.S.T.C. citation for this latter decision.

17.     Source: C.C.H. *Federal Estate & Gift Tax Reporter Citator.* Give as shown the Tax Court citation to the Estate of *Mary H. Hays v. Commissioner.* What did the Fifth Circuit, Court of Appeals do to the original Tax Court decision?

18.     Source: C.C.H. *Federal Estate & Gift Tax Reporter Citator.* The case of *Estate of Carrie Grossman,* was decided by the Tax Court. Give the volume and page citation as shown for this decision. Cite also the 1970 Revenue Ruling which later referred to this *Grossman* decision.

19.     Source: C.C.H. *Federal Estate & Gift Tax Reporter Citator.* Give as shown the citation to the Court of Claims case, *Stewart P. Verckler, Exr (Estate of M.S. Verckler) v. U.S.* In 1962 the *Lorenz* case in the Court of Appeals cited the *Verckler* decision. How was this reference to the *Lorenz* case set out in the citator?

## ASSIGNMENT 3

## THEME PROBLEMS AND DRILL PROBLEMS

**Theme Problem I:**

Many of the cases on discrimination that followed the Brown decision related to discrimination in labor. One of the most comprehensive, and to some, complex looseleaf services is the BNA *Labor Relations Reporter.* Using the full set of this looseleaf, answer the following:

1.  At what page and paragraph does the text of North Dakota labor laws begin?

2.  What is the address of the Idaho Commission on Human Rights? (Hint -- it serves as the state's fair employment practice agency).

3.  What case appears at 18 Fair Employment Practice Cases 966?

4.  Where could one find the text of the Age Discrimination Act of 1975?

**Drill Problem I:**

Using the 2009 CCH *Standard Federal Tax Reporter* and the latest edition of *The Bluebook,* answer the following and properly cite to the looseleaf.

1.  Is a nonresident alien individual who is a member of a partnership which is engaged in business in the U.S. considered to be engaged in business in the U.S.? (CCH)

2.  Where can one find commentary on the taxability of prizes and awards? (CCH)

3.  Cite a case where a taxpayer's contributions to antiwar groups were not allowed as charitable contributions because a large part of the organization's activities were political. (CCH)

**Drill Problem II:**

Using the 2009 CCH *Standard Federal Tax Reporter,* answer the following, indicating the paragraph number at which the answer is located.

     1.     Where can one find Reg. § 1.441-1(T) on the period for computation of taxable income? (CCH)

     2.     Where is there an explanation of the deduction of expenses for education? (CCH)

# Chapter 15

# CITATORS

## ASSIGNMENT 1

### USE OF SHEPARD'S FEDERAL STATUTE CITATIONS CONSTITUTION

Method:

Refer to *Shepard's, Federal Statute Citations, United States Constitution.* Use bound volumes only. Answer the following questions with reference to the United States Constitution sections listed below. Cite as given in *Shepard's.*

    (1)    Give the most recent citation to the official reporter of the Supreme Court of the United States which discussed the section (and clause).

    (2)    Give the latest *A.L.R., A.L.R. Federal* or *Lawyers' Edition* annotation in which the section (and clause) was noted.

**Questions**:

1.    Art. 1, §8, cl. 10

2.    Art. 1, §8, cl. 14

3.    Art. I, §8, cl. 18

4.    Art. II, §1, cl. 2

5.    Art. III, §2, cl. 3

6.    Art. IV

7.    Art. IV, §1

8.    Art. IV, §2

9.    Art. V

10.    Art. VI

11.    Art. VI, cl. 2

12.    Amend. XI

13.    Amend. III

14.    Amend. VII

15.    Amend. VIII

16.    Amend. IX

17.    Amend. X

18.    Amend. XII

19.    Amend. XIV, §5

20.    Amend. XV

21.    Amend. XV, §1

22.    Amend. XVII

23.    Amend XXIV

24.    Amend. XXV

25.    Amend. XXVI

# ASSIGNMENT 2

## USE OF SHEPARD'S FEDERAL STATUTE CITATIONS - 1994 CODE

**Method:**

Refer to *Shepard's Federal Statute Citations, Code Section.* Use bound volumes *only.* Answer the following questions with reference to the 1994 *United States Code* sections listed below. Cite as given in *Shepard's.*

(1)     Has the constitutionality of this statute ever been in question? If so, give the holding and the citation(s) of the case(s) so holding. For references to the Supreme Court of the United States, give only the official reporter.

(2)     Give the latest *A.L.R, A.L.R. Federal* or *Lawyers' Edition* annotation in which the provision was noted.

**Questions:**

1.     Title 1, §109

2.     Title 5, §552a, §d, subd. 3

3.     Title 7, §1 et seq.

4.     Title 8, §1324

5.     Title 10, §125

6.     Title 12, §1829b

7.     Title 15, §15c

8.     Title 18, §13

9.     Title 18, §956

10.    Title 19, §160, §a

11.    Title 20, §236 et seq.

12.    Title 22, §611, §j

13.      Title 23, §131, §e

14.      Title 25, §464

15.      Title 26, §151 et seq.

16.      Title 26, §214

17.      Title 28, §1348

18.      Title 29, §219

19.      Title 30, §811

20.      Title 30, §275

21.      Title 33, §403

22.      Title 35, §122

23.      Title 40, §270d

24.      Title 42, §607

25.      Title 47, §315, §a

## ASSIGNMENT 3

## USE OF STATE SHEPARD'S

**Method:**

Refer to the *Shepard's* citator for your state. Use the bound volumes only unless the subject section of the information required can be located only in the temporary supplement to the bound volumes. Cite as given in *Shepard's*.

**Questions:**

1.  Locate the section in your state citator covering your state's probate code. Select one article or section and answer the following questions:
    (a)  Has it been amended, repealed, etc.? If so, answer with the latest citation as given in *Shepard's*.
    (b)  Has it been discussed in a legal periodical? If so, answer with citation as given in *Shepard's*.
    (c)  If available, give the citation to the latest attorney general's opinion citing this article or section.

2.  Locate the section in your state citator covering your state's code of criminal procedure. Select one article or section and answer the following questions:
    (a)  Give the citation (*National Reporter System* and official, if available) to the latest case citing this article or section.
    (b)  Has it been amended, repealed, etc.? If so, give the latest citation as given in *Shepard's*.

3.  Locate the section in your state citator covering the *Uniform Commercial Code.* Select one article and section and answer the following questions:
    (a)  Has it been amended or repealed by the state legislature? If so, in what year?
    (b)  Give the latest legal periodical citation to this section.

4.  Locate the section containing the official reports of the highest court of your state. Select one case from the earliest bound volume of your state's citator. "Shepardize" the case through all subsequent volumes by answering the following questions:

(a)    What is the *National Reporter System* citation to the same case?

(b)    Give the citation of the case if it is reprinted in another reporter.

(c)    Was the case appealed to the Supreme Court of the United States? If so, what was the result? Give the official citation only.

(d)    Has the holding of the case been criticized, distinguished, overruled, etc., by later decisions? Have these later cases cited the total case or only certain principles? In you answer, designate headnote numbers where necessary.

(e)    Has the opinion been cited by the attorney general of your state? If so, give the latest citation.

(f)    Has the cited opinion been noted in an *A.L.R.* annotation? If so, give the latest citation.

(g)    Has the case been cited in any legal periodicals?  If so, give the citation(s).

5.    Locate the section in your state citator containing the *National Reporter System* regional reporter for your area. Select one case and answer the following questions:

(a)    What is the official citation to the same case?

(b)    Has the case been overruled? If so, cite the overruling case.

6.    Locate the section in your state citator containing the Table of Acts by Popular Names or Short Titles. Select one act and answer the following:

(a)    What is citation of the act?

(b)    Are amendments to the act listed in the Table?

7.    Locate the section in your state citator covering the rules of the highest court. Select one rule and answer the following questions:

(a)    Has the rule been amended? If so, cite the source where the amendment can be found.

(b)    Has the highest court of your state ever cited this rule? If so, give the citation to the first case citing this rule.

(c)    Has the rule been cited in any legal periodicals? If so, give the citation(s) to the periodical(s).

(d)    Has this rule been cited in any *A.L.R.* annotation? If so, cite the annotation(s).

8.      Locate the section in your state citator covering municipal ordinances or charters.
   (a)      From the index to charters determine how many municipalities have been involved in litigation involving public utility rates.
   (b)      Select one municipality from the previous question 8(a). Give all citations pertaining to one ordinance or charter provision.

9.      Locate the section in your state citator covering the rules of your state bar. Select one rule and answer the following questions:
   (a)      Has the constitutionality of this rule ever been questioned? If so, give all citations to that opinion.
   (b)      Give the citation *(National Reporter System* and official, if available) to the latest case citing this rule.
   (c)      Has the rule been discussed in legal periodicals? If so, cite one.

# ASSIGNMENT 4

## USE OF SHEPARD'S UNITED STATES CITATIONS -- CASE EDITION

**Method**:

Refer to *Shepard's United States Citations, Case Edition*. Use bound volumes of the *Case Edition* do not use any bound supplement volumes. Cite as given in *Shepard's*. Answer the following questions with reference to the cases listed below.

(1)     Give the parallel citation *(Lawyers' Edition, Supreme Court Reporter* and selected case reporters) for the same case.

(2)     Give the citation(s) to the same case in lower courts and/or the United States Supreme Court.

(3)     Has this case been cited by the California Supreme Court? If so, give the most recent cite.

(4)     Has the case been cited in an *Columbia Law Review* article? If so, cite the most recent reference.

**Questions**:

1.     420 U.S. 283

2.     414 U.S. 395

3.     401 U.S. 82

4.     378 U.S. 478

5.     414 U.S. 168

6.     400 U.S. 309

7.     354 U.S. 449

8.     383 U.S. 541

9.     315 U.S. 501

10.     323 U.S. 471

11.    394 U.S. 721

12.    322 U.S. 292

13.    344 U.S. 183

14.    319 U.S. 182

15.    367 U.S. 488

16.    400 U.S. 25

17.    346 U.S. 235

18.    391 U.S. 123

19.    346 U.S. 389

20.    339 U.S. 460

# ASSIGNMENT 5

## USE OF SHEPARD'S FEDERAL CITATIONS -- FEDERAL REPORTER

**Method:**

Refer to *Shepard's Federal Citations, Federal Reporter.* Use the 1995 bound volumes only. Do not use any supplements. Answer the following with reference to the cases listed below. Each citation is followed by a Topic and Key Number form the *Federal Reporter* syllabus to the cited case. This identifies a specific numbered headnote in the cited case. Examine the cited case in the *Federal Reporter,* and identify the *headnote number.*

(1) Give the federal cases that *distinguished* this specific point of law of the cited case by subsequent decisions. Give only *Federal Reporter* and *Federal Supplement* citations. Cite as given in *Shepard's,* but omit the superior numbers in your answers.

(2) List the opinions that relate to the specific headnote but have no analytical symbol preceding the citation. Give only the *most recent Federal Reporter* and/or *Federal Supplement* citations. Cite as given in *Shepard's,* but omit the superior numbers in your answers.

**Questions:**

1. 458 F.2d 1323. Courts - Key #284

2. 398 F.2d 722. Labor Relations - Key #574

3. 413 F.2d 459. Criminal Law - Key #517.1(1)

4. 456 F.2d 112. Civil Rights - Key #43, 44(1)

5. 453 F.2d 54. Schools and school districts - Key #172

6. 442 F.2d 698. Criminal Law - Key #304(1)

7. 430 F.2d 771. Constitutional Law - Key #272, Prisons - Key #13

8. 453 F.2d 661. Criminal Law - Key #1213

9.     450 F.2d 199. Grand Jury - Key #36

10.    371 F.2d 911. Habeas Corpus - Key #59

11.    295 F.2d 531. Criminal Law - Key #823(5)

12.    330 F.2d 859. Federal Civil Procedure - Key #1960

13.    333 F.2d 535. Criminal Law - Key #275

14.    105 F.2d 331. Monopolies - Key #28(6)

15.    171 F. 305. Corporations - Key #560

## ASSIGNMENT 6

## USE OF SHEPARD'S FEDERAL CITATIONS --
## FEDERAL SUPPLEMENT, FEDERAL RULES DECISIONS,
## COURT OF CLAIMS

**Method:**

Refer to *Shepard's Federal Citations: Federal Supplement, Federal Rules Decisions, Court of Claims.* Use 1995 edition bound volumes only. Answer the following questions with reference to the cases listed below. Cite as given in *Shepard's.*

(1)     Was the cited case appealed to a United States Court of Appeals? If the action of the court is indicated (e.g., affirmed, dismissed, modified, reversed) specify the action and give the latest citation to the *National Reporter System.*

(2)     Was the cited case appealed to the Supreme Court of the United States? If the action of the Court is indicated. (e.g., affirmed, dismissed, modified, reversed) specify the action and give the latest citation to the official reporter.

(3)     Give the latest A.L.R., *A.L.R. Federal or Lawyers' Edition* annotation in which the cited case was noted. Disregard superior numbers.

**Questions:**

1.     3 F. Supp. 909

2.     29 F. Supp. 436

3.     38 Ct. Cl. 10

4.     30 F. Supp. 570

5.     30 F.R.D. 3

6.     235 F. Supp. 183

7.     59 Ct. Cl. 593

8.     2 F.R.D. 270

9.      192 F. Supp. 170

10.     87 F. Supp. 691

11.     136 Ct. Cl. 324

17.     200 F. Supp. 653

13.     99 Ct. Cl. 1

14.     37 F.R.D. 330

15.     236 F. Supp. 56

16.     21 F.R.D. 335

17.     342 F. Supp. 616

18.     191 Ct. Cl. 191

19.     43 F.R.D. 308

20.     21 F.R.D. 335

# ASSIGNMENT 7

## USE OF SHEPARD'S UNITED STATES STATUTES AT LARGE

**Method:**

Refer to *Shepard's Federal Statutes Citations*, United States Statutes at Large, 1996 (not included in the *United States Code*) Section. Use bound volumes only. Answer the following questions with reference to the sections of the *Statutes at Large* which are not included in the *United States Code* listed below. Cite as given in *Shepard's.*

(1 ) Cite any act of Congress noted as affecting this statute and briefly give the effect (e.g., amended, repealed, etc.) of such act.

(2) Give the latest citing of the statute by the Supreme Court of the United States. Give the official reporter citation only.

**Questions:**

1. 1789, July 4, ch. 2, §1, 1 Stat. 24

2. 1809, March 1, ch. 24, 2 Stat. 528

3. 1870, May 31, ch. 114, §4, 16 Stat. 140

4. 1875, Feb. 8, ch. 36, § 18, 18 Stat. 307

5. 1921, May 19, ch. 8, 42 Stat. 5

6. 1927, Jan. 21, ch. 47, §1, 44 Stat. 1010

7. 1935, Aug. 30, ch. 829, §105, 49 Stat. 1014

8. 1940, July 2, ch. 508, §1, 54 Stat. 712

9. 1948, April 3, ch. 169, §101, 62 Stat. 137

10. 1958, July 7, P.L. 85-508, §4, 72 Stat. 339

11. 1789, July 4, ch. 2, 1 Stat. 24

12.    1801, Feb. 27, ch. 15, 2 Stat. 103

13.    1836, April 20, ch. 54, 5 Stat. 10

14.    1889, Jan. 14, ch. 24, 25 Stat. 642

15.    1901, March 3, ch. 854, §823, 31 Stat. 1189

16.    1906, June 20, ch. 3446, §2, 34 Stat. 316

17.    1959, Sept. 14, P.L. 86-272, § 201, 73 Stat. 555

18.    1897, June 7, ch. 3, §1, 30 Stat. 62

19.    1919, Oct. 28, ch. 85, 41 Stat. 305

# ASSIGNMENT 8

## USE OF SHEPARD'S REGIONAL REPORTER CITATIONS

**Method:**

Refer to *Shepard's Regional Reporter Citations.* Use bound volumes only. Answer the following questions with reference to the cases listed below. Cite as given in *Shepard's.*

(1) Give the official citation of the case.

(2) Has the cited case been appealed to the Supreme Court of the United States? If appealed, give the official reporter citation.

(3) Do any of *Shepard's* symbols indicate that the cited case has been overruled by subsequent decisions?

(4) List all other states and the District of Columbia which have cited this opinion.

**Questions:**

1. 201 A.2d 715

2. 182 A.2d 596

3. 66 N.E.2d 888

4. 95 N.W.2d 273

5. 10 P.2d 597

6. 61 P.2d 293

7. 106 P.2d 755

8. 237 S.W. 786

9. 244 S.W. 549

10. 78 S.E.2d 462

11. 86 S.E.2d 114

12.     155 So.2d 586

13.     252 A.2d 580

14.     198 N.E.2d 590

15.     34 N.W. 1

16.     69 P. 564

17.     393 S.W.2d 739

18.     260 A.2d 68

19.     241 A.2d 691

20.     221 N.E.2d 543

21.     183 N.E.2d 579

22.     78 N.W.2d 509

23.     192 N.W.2d 466

24.     450 P.2d 775

25.     416 P.2d 67

26.     124 S.E. 2d 653

27.     108 S.E.2d 328

28.     243 S.W.2d 683

29.     523 S.W.2d 377

30.     93 So.2d 769

# ASSIGNMENT 9

## USE OF SHEPARD'S ACTS AND CASES BY POPULAR NAMES

## Method:

Refer to *Shepard's Acts and Cases by Popular Names.* Use 1999 bound volume. Answer the following questions. Cite as given in *Shepard's.*

## Questions:

1.  (a)  Give the citation for the Golden Nematode Act.
    (b)  When was it enacted?

2.  How many states have enacted Sunday Observance Acts?

3.  What is the U.S. Supreme Court citation for the Busing case?

4.  Give the citation to the Watergate Tapes Case.

5.  Where can the Fugitive Slave Law case be found?

6.  Give citations to the Pocahontas Case.

7.  Give citations to the Negligent Attorney case.

8.  Cite Oklahoma's Law Library Act.

9.  What government administrative agency ruled on the Station Facilities case? Cite the agency report of the case.

10.  Give the citations to the latest U.S. Supreme Court reports on the Girard College Cases.

11.  How many states have No-Knock Acts? Give citations to these acts.

12.  Give the citation to the Colorado Ute Indian Water Rights Settlement Act.

13.  (a)  Give the citation for the Citizens Abroad Act.
     (b)  When was it enacted?

14.	Give the citation to the Theatrical Productions Case.

15.	How many states have adopted a Sidewalk Cafe Act?

16.	Give the citation to the earliest enactment of the Removal of Causes Acts.

18.	Give the citation to the Municipal Railway Election case.

18.	How many "Mutt and Jeff" cases have been reported?

19.	Give the citations to the Milk, Cream and Butterfat case.

20.	Give the citations to the Moldy Tomato Paste case.

21.	Give the citation to the latest Mutual Security Act of 1960.

22.	Give the citation to the Horsemeat and Pet Food Act.

23.	Has Nebraska enacted an Air-Raid Precautions Act?

24.	Give the citation to the official report of the U.S. Supreme Court in the Federal Maternity Act case.

25.	Give the citation to the Fowler Hotel case.

26.	Give the citations to the Bob-Tail case.

27.	Give the citation to the Butterfly Jewel Case.

28.	Give the citations to the Cutler case.

29.	Give the citations to the Rat case.

30.	(a)	Was the Betty Boop case heard before the U.S. Supreme Court?
	(b)	Give the citation to the first reported opinion in the Betty Boop case.

31.	Give the citation to the Mystic River Dam Loan Act.

32.	Give the citation for the Electric Companies Act.

33.   Give the latest citation to the Forty-Three Gallons of Cognac Brandy case.

34.   How many states have adopted an Indian Arts and Crafts Sales Act?

35.   Which state passed the 1979-1980 Home Heating Oil Emergency Credit Act?

## ASSIGNMENT 10

## THEME AND DRILL PROBLEMS

**Theme Problem I:**

Find the place that the *Brown* decision (347 U.S. 483) first appears in *Shepard's United States Citations--Cases Edition* and, using that volume, answer the following questions:

1. Give the parallel citations.

2. What Missouri cases cite *Brown*?

3. Where in 373 U.S. is *Brown* cited in dissent?

4. What Alabama cases cite *Brown*?

5. Where was *Brown* cited in 401 U.S.?

6. Has it been overruled?

7. What Florida case in 342 So.2d cites it?

8. Where in 433 U.S. is it followed?

**Theme Problem II:**

Locate the first appearance of *Roe v. Wade,* 410 U.S. 113, in *Shepard's United States Citations--Case Edition* and, using that volume, answer the following questions;

1. Give the parallel citations.

2. Where is the denial of a rehearing reported?

3. What South Dakota case cites it?

4. What Federal District Court opinions "harmonize" it?

5. Has it been overruled?

6. Where in 431 U.S. is it distinguished?

**Theme Problem III:**

Find the first appearance of *Gideon v. Wainwright,* 372 U.S. 335, in *Shepard's United States Citations--Case Edition* and, using that volume, answer the following questions:

    1.        Give the parallel citations.

    2.        What is the first time it is cited in dissent?

    3.        What is the first Idaho decision listed?

    4.        Has it been overruled or reversed?

    5.        Where is the first time the decision is "explained"?

    6.        What is the first Arkansas decision cited?

    7.        Where is it cited in 433 U.S.?

    8.        Where is it cited in 265 N.W.2d?

**Drill Problem I:**

A.      Using only bound volumes of *Shepard's United States Citations--Case Edition* (do not use any bound supplements), answer the following questions for each of the citations listed below:

    (1)     What is the first case listed that cited the decision in dissent?
    (2)     Give the parallel citations.
    (3)     Has the case been reversed or overruled?

    1.       397 U.S. 249

    2.       406 U.S. 441

    3.       93 S.Ct. 2405

B.      Using only bound volumes of *Shepard's Federal Citations--Cases* (do not use any bound supplements), answer the following questions for each citation listed below:

    (1)     List the first case cited from the 1st circuit, if any.

(2)    List the first case listed that followed the decision.

(3)    Has it been reversed or overruled?

(4)    If there is an *A.L.R.* citation, list it.

1.    469 F.2d 1377

2.    496 F.2d 1303

3.    220 F. 545

C.    Using only bound volumes of the regional *Shepard's,* answer the following questions for each citation listed below:

(1)    List the first case that cites the decision in dissent.

(2)    Cite the first regional reporter case listed.

(3)    Give the parallel citation.

(4)    Has the decision been reversed?

1.    71 P. 453

2.    208 S.E.2d 459

3.    131 N.W.2d 293

D.    Using the 1996 bound volumes of *Shepard's Federal Statute Citations,* answer the following questions *for each citation listed below:*

(1)    Give the first U.S. Supreme Court citation listed, if any.

(2)    Has its constitutionality been adjudicated? If yes, list the first citation.

(3)    Give the first *A.L.R. Federal* citation listed.

1.    42 U.S.C. § 3613

2.    10 U.S.C. § 1552

3.    12 U.S.C. § 1768

E.    Using the 1996 bound volume of *Shepard's Federal Statutes Citations -- U.S. Constitution,* answer the following questions for each citation listed below:

(1)    Give the first citation to a U.S. Supreme Court case, if any.

(2)    Give first citation to *A.L.R.,* if any.

(3) Any special action (i.e., amended) noted? If so, provide first citation.

1. Art. III, §1

2. Art. II, §1

**Drill Problem II:**

A. Using only bound volumes of *Shepard's United States Citations-Case Edition* (do not use any bound supplements), answer the following questions for each citation listed below:

(1) What is the first case listed that cited the decision in dissent?
(2) Give the parallel citations.
(3) Has the case been reversed or overruled?

1. 360 U.S. 264

2. 403 U.S. 388

3. 36 L.E.2d 366

B. Using only bound volumes of *Shepard's Federal Citations--Cases* (do not use any bound supplements), answer the following questions for each citation listed below:

(1) List the first case cited from the 1st Circuit.
(2) List the first case listed that followed the decision.
(3) Has it been reversed or overruled?
(4) If there is an *A.L.R.* cite, list it.

1. 415 F.2d 1185

2. 505 F.2d 977

3. 67 F.2d 585

4. 323 F. Supp. 799

C. Using only bound volumes of the regional *Shepard's*, answer the following questions for each citation listed below:

(1)     List the first case that cites the decision in dissent.
(2)     Cite the first regional reporter case listed.
(3)     Give the parallel citation.
(4)     Has the decision been reversed?

1.      34 P.2d 534

2.      1 So. 273

3.      256 N.E.2d 384

D.      Using the 1996 bound volumes of *Shepard's Federal Statutes Citations --
U.S. Code 1994,* answer the following questions for each citation listed below:

(1)     Give the first U.S. Supreme Court citation listed, if any.
(2)     Has its constitutionality been adjudged? If yes, list the first citation.
(3)     Give the First *A.L.R. Fed.* citation listed.

1.      33 U.S.C. §407

2.      45 U.S.C. §153(1)(p)

E.      Using the 1996 bound volumes of *Shepard's Federal Statutes Citations --
U.S. Constitution,* answer the following questions for each citation listed below:

(1)     Give the first citation to a U.S. Supreme Court case, if any.
(2)     Give first citation to *A.L.R.,* if any.
(3)     Any special action (i.e., amended) noted? If so, provide first
        citation.

1.      Amendment IX

2.      Amendment XVIII

**Drill Problem III:**

A.      Using only bound volumes of *Shepard's United States Citations--Case
Edition* (do not use any bound supplements), answer the following questions for
each citation listed below:

(1)     What is the first case listed that cited the decision in dissent?
(2)     Give the parallel citations.

    (3)       Has the case been reversed or overruled?

    1.        346 U.S. 1

    2.        397 U.S. 471

    3.        256 U.S. 135

B.      Using only bound volumes of *Shepard's Federal Citations - Cases* (do not use any bound supplements), answer the following questions for each citation listed below:

    (1)       List the first case cited from the 1st Circuit.
    (2)       List the first case listed that followed the decision.
    (3)       Has it been reversed or overruled?
    (4)       If there is an *A.L.R.* citation, list it.

    1.        471 F.2d 488

    2.        185 F.2d 622

    3.        62 F. Supp. 73

    4.        340 F. Supp. 1343

C.      Using the appropriate bound volume of regional *Shepard's -- Cases,* answer the following questions for each citation listed below:

    (1)       List the first case that cites the decision in dissent.
    (2)       Cite the first regional reporter case listed.
    (3)       Give the parallel citation.
    (4)       Has the decision been reversed?

    1.        236 S.W.2d 772

    2.        337 A.2d 893

    3.        181 N.W.2d 811

D.      Using the 1996 bound volumes to *Shepard's Federal Statute Citations,* answer the following questions for each citation listed below:

    (1)       Give the first U.S. Supreme Court citation listed, if any.

(2)     Has its constitutionality been adjudged? If yes, list the first citation.

(3)     Give the first *A.L.R. Fed.* citation listed.

1.     18 U.S.C. §2520

2.     28 U.S.C. §2111

3.     82 Stat. 815

E.     Using the 1996 bound volumes of *Shepard's Federal Statutes Citations -- U.S. Constitution,* answer the following questions for each citation listed below:

(1)     Give the first citation to a U.S. Supreme Court case, if any.

(2)     Give first citation to A.L.R., if any.

(3)     Any special action (i.e., amended) noted? If so, provide first citation.

1.     Art. 1, §6, cl. 1

2.     Amendment 1

# Chapter 16

# LEGAL ENCYCLOPEDIAS

## ASSIGNMENT 1

### THE INDEX METHOD WITH AMERICAN JURISPRUDENCE 2d AND CORPUS JURIS SECUNDUM

**Method:**

Analyze each of the following problems for words, expressed or implied, which should be in the general index or specific volume index of the encyclopedia abbreviated in the parenthesis following each problem. A completed answer to each problem should contain the following parts:

(1)  A tentative answer to the legal problems;
(2)  Word(s) in the index under which the encyclopedic text was found;
(3)  Identification of index in which word was found (i.e., "volume index" or "general index");
(4)  Citation to the encyclopedic text in which the tentative answer was discovered.

This citation should be expressed in the form set out in the latest edition of A *The Bluebook.*

**Example:**

|  |  |
|---|---|
| QUESTION: | Are rental houses not held for sale, subject to depreciation under federal taxation laws? (Am. Jur. 2d) |
| ANSWER: | (1)  Yes |
|  | (2)  Deductions- eligibility for |
|  | (3)  Volume index |
|  | (4)  33 Am. Jur. 2d *Federal Taxation* §14055 (2007). |

**Questions:**

1. In a civil proceeding aimed at removal of environmental pollution is a preponderance of the evidence sufficient to establish violation of statute? (C.J.S.).

2. Was the Korean conflict a war in the constitutional or legal sense? (Am. Jur. 2d).

3. Did the Nineteenth Amendment confer upon women the right to vote? (C.J.S.)

4. According to recent authority, in a juvenile court proceeding, are juveniles entitled to constitutional protection against twice being placed in jeopardy for the same offense? (Am. Jur. 2d).

5. Can a court take judicial notice of standard mortality tables? (C.J.S.).

6. Does a person who enters the military service lose thereby the domicile which he had before he entered the service? (Am. Jur. 2d).

7. In a trial, must the plaintiff ordinarily establish his prima facie case before cross-examination of defendant's witnesses? (C.J.S.).

8. Is a student at a state college entitled to notice and hearing before being expelled for misconduct? (Am. Jur. 2d).

9. May a person, who has a right to treat an absolute deed as a mortgage, lose the right through laches, or prejudicial delay? (C.J.S.).

10. If a woman agrees to care for and nurse a man for the rest of his life in return for his promise to will her all his property, will their agreement be invalidated by their future illicit cohabitation? (C.J.S.).

11. Are punchboards exempted from the federal wagering taxes? (Am. Jur. 2d).

12. Is competition an essential element of the offense of "drag racing?" (C.J.S.).

13. Does a parent's failure to support his child by itself constitute such abandonment, desertion or neglect which would permit adoption without the parent's consent? (C.J.S.).

14. In order to challenge a juror for cause based upon bias or prejudice may the juror be examined concerning his relationships with parties to the action, counsel, prospective witnesses, or other persons interested in the action who are not parties of record? (C.J.S.).

15. May a court disbar an attorney for defamatory criticisms of judicial acts incorporated in a brief? (Am. Jur. 2d).

16. Is a district or prosecuting attorney of a state entitled to extra compensation when he has a duty to perform services in another county in connection with a suit to which his county is a party? (C.J.S.).

17. May the family purpose doctrine be applied to impose tort liability for personal injury on a family corporation which owns the automobile in question and maintains it for general family use? (C.J.S.).

18 Will a tenant at sufferance be liable to his landlord for an injury to the premises which was caused by a fire resulting from the tenant's negligence? (C.J.S.).

19. Does public policy require that a state recognize a bilateral Mexican divorce as a matter of comity? (Am. Jur. 2d).

20. Must other vessels exercise care to avoid a collision with a vessel which has obstructed a narrow channel? (C.J.S.).

21. Is an infant liable on the basis of quasi-contract for the value of necessaries furnished him? (Am. Jur. 2d).

22. Is a state barred from making payment of a poll tax a prerequisite to voting? (Am Jur. 2d).

23. Is the concealment in a licensing proceeding of a prior arrest record a ground for the refusal of an application for a license to sell intoxicating liquors? (Am. Jur. 2d).

24. Does a passenger voluntarily assume a risk with respect to a commercial plane itself and its operation? (C.J.S.).

25. May a material false statement made under oath in connection with an application for a marriage license constitute perjury? (Am. Jur. 2d).

26. If a factory has made advances on consigned goods, is he bound to accept and pay a draft drawn on him by the principal before the advances are repaid? (C.J.S.)

27. Does the federal crime of seditious conspiracy require an overt act for its completion? (Am. Jur. 2d).

28. Is the manufacture of meat products from horse meat illegal as a violation of a regulation prohibiting the manufacture for sale of adulterated food if there is no attempt to conceal the fact the product is horse meat? (C.J.S.).

29. Does a builder have an obligation to perform extra work without compensation if that work is not specified in the construction plans which themselves form a part of the contract? (C.J.S.).

30. Have courts found that the freedom of religion of Jewish persons is violated by Sunday closing laws? (Am. Jur. 2d).

31. Under the Lanham Act, will the type of product for which a trademark is to be registered affect whether or not the mark is considered scandalous? (C.J.S.).

32. Do the statutes regulating telephone companies include within their scope the operation of a two-way mobile radio system? (Am. Jur. 2d).

33. Can a false misrepresentation be implied from the exhibiting of fraudulent or misleading maps or plats? (Am. Jur. 2d).

# ASSIGNMENT 2

## USE OF THE TOPIC METHOD WITH AMERICAN JURISPRUDENCE 2d AND CORPUS JURIS SECUNDUM

**Method:**

Analyze each of the problems below for words, expressed or implied, to determine the suggested topic(s). Using the encyclopedia indicated in the parenthesis following each problem, turn to the topic's "analysis" or list of major subject divisions and then to the more detailed "sub-analysis" or section outline. Your answer should contain the following information:

(1)　Answer to the legal problem posed.
(2)　A citation to the encyclopedic text in which the answer was found.

Follow the citation form set out in the latest edition of *The Bluebook.*

**Example:**

QUESTION: May an offer of a reward be revoked at any time before it is accepted by performance?

ANSWER　(1)　Yes
　　　　　(2)　67 Am. Jur. 2d *Rewards* §16 (2003).

**Questions:**

1.　May a railroad company acquire title to land by adverse possession or prescription? (C.J.S.).

2.　Does the assignment of the interest of a vendor or vendee in a contract for the sale of land as security for a debt create an equitable mortgage? (C.J.S.).

3.　Is the Securities and Exchange Commission authorized to subpoena witnesses and to require the production of relevant books, papers and documents? (C.J.S.).

4       Does mere inaction constitute negligence where a duty has been undertaken gratuitously? (C.J.S.).

5.      Can a municipal corporation be held civilly liable for its failure to enact or enforce ordinances? (C.J.S.).

6.      May the crime of forgery be committed by the signing of a fictitious or assumed name? (Am. Jur. 2d).

7.      Are unavoidably unsafe products classified as unreasonably dangerous for purposes of the strict liability doctrine when they are accompanied by proper directions and warnings? (Am. Jur. 2d).

8.      May a state ever take or authorize the taking of property situated in another state under its powers of eminent domain? (Am. Jur. 2d).

9.      Must an overt act be of a criminal nature in order to warrant conviction for treason? (Am. Jur. 2d).

10.     May a false statement on an income tax return constitute perjury? (Am. Jur. 2d).

11.     Is the offense of fraudulent enlistment in the military service exclusively a military offense punishable only by court-martial? (Am. Jur. 2d).

12.     May a corporation legally change or alter the name originally selected by it without recourse to formal proceedings? (Am. Jur. 2d).

13.     Can a change in the law render a contract illegal which was legal when made? (C.J.S.).

14.     Does the law impose on the bailee the duty of insuring the subject matter of the bailment? (C.J.S.).

15.     Will refusal to permit challenges and watchers to be present at the polls, during the conduct of an election, invalidate the election? (C.J.S.).

16. May the release of mutual claims by each of two persons constitute an accord and satisfaction? (C.J.S.).

17. In order to constitute an escrow must the deposit be irrevocable? (Am. Jur. 2d).

18. May a failure, with excuse, to obey a court order to pay money, constitute contempt? (C.J.S.).

19. Is a wife obliged to furnish her husband with a home, if she had one and he does not have a home? (Am. Jur. 2d).

20. May a will be revoked by oral declaration? (C.J.S.).

21. Does a state Sunday closing law violate the U.S. Constitution respecting establishment of religion, where the present purpose and effect of the statute is not to aid religion, but to set aside a day of rest and recreation? (Am. Jur. 2d).

22. Is a state statute prohibiting desertion and nonsupport of unborn children valid? (Am. Jur. 2d).

23. Is a contract for the sale of standing timber within the Statute of Frauds? (C.J.S.).

24. May a qualified expert testify from the nature of a wound as to the character of the weapon which inflicted or could have inflicted the wound? (Am. Jur. 2d).

25. Is the state regarded as a party to every divorce proceeding? (C.J.S.).

26. Will the court grant a decree of specific performance of a binding oral contract? (Am. Jur. 2d).

27. Will jurisdiction for a declaratory judgment be entertained where another equally appropriate remedy is already available? (C.J.S.).

28. May a person maintain a proceeding for a variance from a zoning law, if his sole purpose is to obtain a higher valuation in condemnation proceedings? (C.J.S.).

29.   Is an employer prohibited by law from discriminatory actions to discourage or encourage service as a union steward? (Am. Jur. 2d).

30.   May a beneficiary under a trust deed foreclose a mortgage on the trust property, when the trustee neglects to do so? (C.J.S.)

# ASSIGNMENT 3

## DRILL PROBLEMS FOR LEGAL ENCYCLOPEDIAS

### Instructions:

For each of the following questions:
(1)     provide a "yes" or "no" answer;
(2)     cite the volume, title and section of the encyclopedia under which the correct answer can be found.

The answer should be in proper citation form according to the latest edition of *The Bluebook.*

### Drill Problem I:

A.      Use C.J.S. to answer the following questions:

1.      Are children born of parents who are subject to jurisdiction of a country considered citizens of that country even if their parents are aliens?

2.      Does simple pursuit of game confer on a hunter a right of ownership?

B.      Use Am. Jur. 2d to answer the following questions:

1.      When a person is sentenced to life imprisonment, can his/her property then be distributed as if death had occurred?

2.      Is an owner who burns his/her house while it is in the possession of another guilty of arson?

### Drill Problem II:

A.      Use C.J.S. to answer the following questions:

1.      Is a statement as to genealogy admissible as an exception to the hearsay rule?

2.      Was the utterance of obscene words in public indictable at common law?

B.     Use Am. Jur. 2d to answer the following questions:

    1.     Have the Courts traditionally viewed the use of threats or force to Recover gambling losses as "robbery?"

    2.     If unruly spectators may have caused prejudice in a trial, can the verdict be appealed?

    3.     Can one find discussion and text of Federal Rules of Evidence? Where?

**Drill Problem III:**

A.     Use C.J.S. to answer the following questions:

    1.     Under negligence theory, if someone habitually trespasses upon your land, does your knowledge of the trespass create a duty of care for the trespasser's safety?

    2.     Can counsel use medical texts on the cross examination of an expert witness?

B.     Use Am. Jur. 2d to answer the following questions:

    1.     Does the act of advertising to treat patients by mail by means of "mental science" show a scheme to use the mails of the United States Post Office for fraud absent any other proof?

    2.     In prosecutions for adultery, does the burden rest upon the state to prove beyond a reasonable doubt every material element of the offense charged, in order to sustain a conviction?

# Chapter 17

# AMERICAN LAW REPORTS

## ASSIGNMENT 1

## ALR INDEX: USE OF THE ALR INDEX TO LOCATE ANNOTATIONS ON POINTS OF LAW

**Method:**

Using the index designated in the following problem sub-sets, locate and cite, using the latest edition of *The Bluebook,* annotations on point for each fact situation provided. You may have to refer to the actual Annotation in order to provide the year in your citation.

**Example:**

| | |
|---|---|
| QUESTION: | A cat as a subject of a larceny. |
| ANSWER: | Annot., 55 A.L.R.4th 1080 (1987) |

**Questions:**

A.     Use the *A.L.R. First Series Quick Index* to locate the following points of law appearing in A.L.R. 1-175.

   1.     Right of exclusion from or discrimination against patrons of library.

   2.     Legality of, and injunction against, peaceful picketing by labor union of plant whose employees are represented by another union as statutory bargaining agent.

   3.     When is an individual deemed an inhabitant of the state within taxing law?

   4.     Liability of insane person for tort.

5. Irresistible impulse as excuse for crime.

6. Correct name of married woman.

7. Civil liability for defamation of the dead.

8. Homicide or assault as ground for disbarment of an attorney.

9. Validity of bequest or trust for care of specified animal.

10. Immoral relations between insured and beneficiary as affecting liability of insurer or interest in proceeds of the policy.

B. Use the *ALR Index* to locate the following points of law appearing in A.L.R.2d 1-100.

1. Presumption of deliberation or premeditation from the fact of killing.

2. Public payment of tuition to a sectarian school.

3. Identification of accused by his voice.

4. Right of the accused to have defense witnesses free from manacles.

5. Rights of fraternal society to protection against the use of its name, insignia, or ritual by another organization.

6. Liability of dentist using force to restrain or discipline patient.

C. Use the *ALR Index* to locate the following points of law appearing in A.L.R.3d 1-100.

1. Common-law copyright in the spoken word.

2. Penal offense of sniffing glue or similar volatile intoxicants.

3. Tenants' rights where landlord fails to make repairs, to have them made and set off cost against rent.

4. Free exercise of religion as a defense to prosecution for narcotic offense.

5. When is a will signed at the "end" or the "foot" as required by statute?

6. Attack on judiciary as a whole as indirect contempt.

7. Public disclosure of person's indebtedness as invasion of privacy.

8. Literary property in lectures.

D. Use the *ALR Index* to locate the following points of law in *A.L.R.4th*.

1. Privileged communications between accountant and client.

2. Products liability: animal feed or medicines.

3. Homicide as precluding taking under will or intestacy.

4. Sufficiency of access to legal research facilities afforded defendant confined in the state prison or local jail.

5. Civil liability for insulting or abusive language—modern status.

6. Regulation of the practice of acupuncture.

7. Attorney's failure to attend court, or tardiness, as contempt.

8. Admissibility of hearsay evidence in probation revocation hearings.

9. Liability for negligent operation of dune buggy.

10. Fact that witness undergoes hypnotic examination as affecting admissibility of testimony in civil case.

11. Modern trends as to tort liability of child of tender years.

12. Recovery by bank of money paid out to customer by mistake.

13. Disclosure or use of computer application software as misappropriation of trade secret.

E.      Use the *ALR Index* to locate the following points of law appearing in
A.L.R. 5th.

1.      Travel organization, liability of travel publication, travel agent or similar party for personal injury or death of traveler.

2.      Right of worker's compensation insurer or employer paying to a worker's compensation fund, on the compensable death of an employee with no dependents to indemnity or subrogation from proceeds or wrongful death action brought against third-party tort-feaser.

3.      Offer of employment, employer's state law liability for withdrawing or substantially altering, job offer before employee actually commences employment.

4.      Vaginal delivery, liability of hospital, physician, or other medical personnel for death or injury to mother or child caused by improper procedures during vaginal delivery.

5.      Expert and opinion evidence, divorce, spouses right to order that other spouse pay expert witness fees.

6.      Contagious or communicable diseases, liability of doctor or other health practitioner to third party contracting contagious disease from doctor's patient.

7.      Guy wires, liability for injury or death from collision with guy wire.

8       Labor and employment, post-delivery care liability of hospital, physician, or other medical personnel for death or injury to post-delivery diagnosis, care, and representations.

9.      Ratification, commodities, compromise of action, ratification of attorney's unauthorized compromise of action.

10.     Vacation and modification of judgment or verdict, jurisdiction, filing of notice of appeal as affecting jurisdiction of state trial court to consider motion to vacate judgment.

F. Use the *ALR Index* to locate the following points of law appearing in A.L.R. Fed.

1. Inability of employer to pay wages and damages as defense to wage order under Fair Labor Standards Act.

2. Authority of Secretary of Army to deny dredging and filling permit for ecological reasons under Sec. 10 of Rivers and Harbors Act of 1899.

3. Making, selling or distributing counterfeit tape recordings' as violation of federal law.

4. Liability of the United States under Federal Tort Claims Act for damages caused by ingestion or administration of drugs and vaccines approved as safe for use by government agency.

5. Right of accused to bill of particulars in criminal prosecution for evasion of federal income taxes.

6. Acquittal or conviction in state court as bar to federal prosecution based on same fact.

7. Right of accused to inspect the minutes of federal grand jury.

8. Application in federal civil action of governmental privilege of nondisclosure of identity of informer.

9. Construction and application of Food Stamp Act of 1964 establishing food stamp program.

10. Discharge from Armed Forces on ground of conscientious objection.

11. Validity and construction of federal statute requiring registration on crossing border of narcotics user.

12. Unauthorized photocopying by library as infringement of copyright.

13. What acts amount to violation of Hatch Political Activities Act provisions against political activities of certain state and local employees?

14.     Construction and application of provision of Freedom of
        Information Act exempting from disclosure personnel and
        medical files.

15.     Sex discrimination in athletics, validity under federal law.

## ASSIGNMENT 2

## USE OF TABLE OF CASES OF WEST'S A.L.R. DIGEST
## TO LOCATE CASE CITATIONS AND ANNOTATIONS

**Method:**

Provide the case citation and the cite to the A.L.R. annotation, omitting dates.

**Example:**

| | |
|---|---|
| QUESTION: | *Dunn v. White* |
| ANSWER: | 206 Kan. 278, 479 P.2d 215, 47 A.L.R.3d 1289 |

**Questions:**

A.     Use the *Permanent A.L.R. Digest* (covering A.L.R. vols.1-175) — Table of Cases.

1.     *Henson v. Henson*

2.     *Keith v. Kilmer*

3.     *Markovitz v. Markovitz*

4.     *Shulkin v. Shulkin*

5.     *Ziehm v. Vale*

6.     *Crabtree v. Crabtree*

7.     *Brown v. Brown*

B.     Use the *A.L.R.2d 1-100 Digest,* Table of Cases volume.

8.     *Johnson v. Johnson*

9.     *Kennedy v. Parrott*

10.     *Agnew v. American Ice Co.*

11.     *Coolidge & Sickler Inc. v. Regn*

12.     *Wilson v. Anderson*

13.    *Cleveland v. Detroit*

14.    *McKinley v. Long*

15.    *Jackson v. Jackson*

## ASSIGNMENT 3

## ALR INDEX:  USE OF THE ALR INDEX TO LOCATE ANNOTATIONS FROM AMERICAN LAW REPORTS (1st, 2d, 3d, 4th, 5th, & Fed.)

**Method:**

Refer to the *ALR Index*. Find the Annotation History Table.  For each of the following annotations cite any supplementing or superseding annotation.  *Do not consult the pocket part.*

**Example:**

|  |  |
|---|---|
| QUESTION: | 2 A.L.R. 1376 |
| ANSWER: | Superseded 45 A.L.R.2d 1296 |

**Questions:**

1.  3 A.L.R. 1130

2.  20 A.L.R. 407

3.  29 A.L.R. 140

4.  18 A.L.R. 197

5.  17 A.L.R. 760

6.  92 A.L.R.2d 421

7.  42 A.L.R.3d 560

8.  75 A.L.R.3d 1000

9.  133 A.L.R. 11

10.  129 A.L.R. 751

11.  90 A.L.R. 1377

12.  22 A.L.R.2d 427

13. 132 A L.R. 679

14. 118 A.L.R. 1357

15. 97 A.L.R. 1197

## ASSIGNMENT 4

## USE OF THE A.L.R.2d DIGEST
## TO LOCATE CASES THAT HAVE BEEN ADDED TO ANNOTATIONS

**Method:**

Refer to the *A.L.R.2d Digest* for each of the following fact situations and cite the case name and the A.L.R.2d Annotation reference that follows the case name.

**Example:**

QUESTION: Bobby Nissan is present when Jay Myron threatens and strikes Roy Martin. Nissan shouts encouragement to Myron to strike Martin again, which Myron does. Martin sues Nissan for the tort of assault and battery.

ANSWER: *Hargis v. Horrine*, 72 A.L.R.2d 1223

**Questions:**

1. Pedro Montez holds commercial "cockfights" or contests between two roosters armed with artificial spurs. Pedro is arrested and charged with cruelty to animals. He contends that cockfighting is a lawful sport.

2. Charlie Speedo fails to stop after the car he is driving strikes a dog. As a matter of law does his action constitute breach of the peace?

3. Donald Durham, a property owner, shoots and kills a trespassing dog. Does he incur civil liability to the owner of the dog?

4. The proprietor of a golf course offers a prize of $5,000 to any member of the public who shoots a hole in one on his golf course and pays $1 for the opportunity. Fred Fortune pays his dollar and shoots a hole in one. The golf course proprietor refuses to pay the $5,000 contending that the contract was invalid as a "gambling" contract.

5. Rosie Reed promises to give her unborn illegitimate child the given name of the putative father in return for his promise to support the child. Is Rosie's promise adequate consideration for a binding contract?

6. Police Officer Robert Rood arrests and imprisons Larry Lane under a mistaken belief that his is the man named in the warrant. Lane sues Rood for false arrest and unlawful imprisonment. Rood alleges as his defense, the lack of malice or improper motive in making the arrest.

7. Charlie Low beats and pursues his wife to a river bank. He tells her to jump or he will push her. Charlie knows she cannot swim and the river is deep. She jumps and drowns. Charlie makes no effort to help her or summon assistance. He is charged with homicide.

8. Alice and Roger, although living apart because of Roger's heavy drinking, were still married at the time of Alice's death. Eric Eager, a mortician, furnishes Alice with the usual funeral. He seeks payment from Roger, who refuses to pay, contending that his liability for the necessaries of his wife ended upon her death.

9. Adolph Sparks seeks to pay his hospitalization insurance premium on the Monday immediately following the last day of his grace period (Sunday). The insurance company cancels his policy and he sues to reinstate the policy.

10. Noe Nardi, a member of an unincorporated labor union, requests to inspect its financial records. The union refuses his request and Nardi seeks a court order.

11. Elsie Dinsmore is the beneficiary of a testamentary trust that stipulates that the entire corpus will be turned over to her at the age of 32 providing that she has not married a Catholic. She challenges this provision in court as contrary to public policy and therefore void.

12. Paul Pope, a pedestrian, is severely injured by the breaking of a plate glass window in the Arista Department Store during a windstorm. Arista denies that its negligence was the proximate cause of the injury, citing the gusty wind as a superseding cause.

13. Willie Hinkle, a burglar, was hurrying home with his loot of cash and jewels when Salty Macha waved a revolver in front of him and said, "This is a stick-up. Give me your money and jewelry." Willie handed over everything he had stolen to Salty. Salty was later apprehended and at his trial for robbery contends that the proceeds of a burglary cannot be the subject of a robbery.

14. Nuns of a Roman Catholic order teach in a public school wearing distinctive religious garb. A local organization seeks a court order to compel them to wear normal lay clothing while engaged in teaching.

15. Herman Yellin is a school teacher who is in arrears in the payment of debt to the Friendly Finance Company. Friendly Finance writes to Yellin's school superintendent stating that Yellin owes them money, that normal collection efforts have failed, and seeks advice as to whether Yellin is able to pay, before taking further action. Yellin sues for libel. Friendly Finance alleges Yellin states no cause of action without a plea of special damage.

16. Susan Bee is severely injured by the negligent driving of Alien Alfa. Susan's minor son Daniel sues Alfa for loss of his mother's care and attention. Alfa denies Daniel Bee has a cause of action.

17. Robert and Marcia marry. Shortly thereafter Robert learns that Marcia had sexual intercourse with other men prior to their marriage. Robert seeks an annulment of their marriage alleging fraud on the part of Marcia in not divulging her previous incontinence to him.

18. Dr. Hall, in the act of removing sutures from the toe of Jane Fern, a 4 year old patient, strikes her to make her lie still. A bruise remains sore for some weeks. Her father brings an action for assault and battery against Dr. Hail on her behalf.

19. John Brown, a farmer, seeing some boys in the act of stealing watermelons from his fields, fires his rifle to frighten them off. He fires toward a wooded area where unknown to him another boy is hiding. The other boy is severely injured and an action is brought against Brown for assault and battery. Brown claims he is not civilly liable as he acted in defense of his property and he did not intend to injure the boy.

20.     Peter Glass, an attorney, is convicted of willful evasion of federal income taxes, a felony. He is disbarred for conviction of an offense involving fraud or moral turpitude. He contends that income tax evasion is not an offense involving fraud or moral turpitude, and that disbarment as opposed to a suspension was excessive.

## ASSIGNMENT 5

### USE OF THE WEST'S A.L.R. DIGEST TO LOCATE ANNOTATIONS ON POINTS OF LAW APPEARING IN A.L.R.2d, 3d, 4th, 5th, 6th AND FEDERAL

**Method:**

Locate and cite, in proper form, the A.L.R. annotation on each of the following points of law.

**Example:**

QUESTION:     Due process of law as violated by statute or ordinance providing for destruction of dogs without notice or hearing.

ANSWER:       Annot., 56 A.L.R.2d 1037 (1957).

**Questions:**

1. Failure of artisan or construction contractor to procure occupational or business license or permit as affecting validity of contract.

2. Civil liability for use of firearm in defense of habitation or property.

3. Landlord's duty under express covenant to rebuild or restore, where property is damaged or destroyed by fire.

4. Fact that gun was unloaded as affecting criminal responsibility.

5. Right of owner of housing development or apartment houses to restrict canvassing, peddling, solicitations of contributions, etc.

6. Alteration of figures indicating amount of check, bill or note without change in written words as forgery.

7. Liability for statement or publication representing plaintiff as cruel to or killer of animals.

8. Truant or attendance officer's liability for assault and battery.

9. Criminal responsibility of husband for rape, or assault to commit rape on wife.

10. Character and duration of tenancy created by entry under invalid or unenforceable lease.

11. Sex discrimination in the United States Armed Forces.

12. Amount of attorneys' fees in matters involving domestic relations.

13. Insulting words addressed directly to police officer as breach of peace or disorderly conduct.

14. Expenses for which condominium association may assess unit owners.

15. Increase in tuition as actionable in suit by student against college or university.

16. Liability in damages for withholding corpse from relatives.

17. Embezzlement, larceny, false pretenses, or allied criminal fraud by partner.

18. Power of court to remove or suspend judge.

19. Validity, construction, and effect of "Sunday closing" or "blue" laws—modern status.

20. Criminal liability for wrongfully obtaining unemployment benefits.

21. What constitutes "property" obtained within extortion statute.

22. Meaning of the term "hotel" as used in zoning ordinance.

23. Interference with radio or television reception as nuisance.

24. Court-authorized permanent or temporary removal of child by parent to foreign country.

25. Picketing court or judge as contempt.

# ASSIGNMENT 6

## A.L.R.2d LATER CASE SERVICE:
## USE OF A.L.R.2d, LATER CASE SERVICE TO LOCATE RELEVANT
## DECISIONS APPEARING SUBSEQUENT TO ANNOTATIONS
## PUBLISHED IN A.L.R.2d

**Method:**

Refer to *A.L.R.2d, Later Case Service*. For each of the following annotations give the name and citation, according to the latest edition of *The Bluebook*, of the described subsequent case. You may have to refer to the actual case you located in order to provide the complete citation.

**Example:**

QUESTION:          14 A.L.R.2d 7. Subsequent common-law marriage does not raise presumption that former marriage terminated in divorce.

ANSWER:          *Lumbermans Mus. Cas. Co. v. Reed*, 84 Ga. App. 541, 66 S.E.2d 360 (1951).

**Questions:**

1.          5 A.L.R.2d 874. Trial court properly awarded counsel fees to city where taxpayer's case so clearly lacked merit that public interest was not clearly vindicated or served by such litigation.

2.          5 A.L.R.2d 1143. Under common law, where offense occurred February 25, 1967 at 4:30 P.M. and defendant was born February 25, 1950 at 6:32 P.M., defendant had reached 17 years of age at time of offense.

3.          6 A.L.R.2d 859. Allegations that divorced wife used alimony payments for alcohol and drugs and had been arrested 50 or more times and confined in jail on many of these occasions did not justify modification of decree for alimony, at least in absence of allegation on part of divorced husband of inability to continue payments or lack of need on part of wife.

4.          64 A.L.R.2d 100. Recovery was allowed for subsequent illness resulting from plaintiff discovering unpackaged prophylactic in

remaining contents of bottle of Coca-Cola after having drunk a portion thereof.

5.    64 A.L.R.2d 301.  Misconduct while practicing law in another state that included among other things borrowing and failing to return books from the county law library warranted denial of admission to bar.

6.    64 A.L.R.2d 600.  Where spectator at pretrial hearing in Black Panther criminal prosecution disrupted proceeding and was summarily adjudged guilty of contempt, judge was not required to refer contempt proceeding to another judge.

7.    78 A.L.R.2d 905.  Results of breathalyzer test were properly suppressed where officer failed to advise defendant of his right to have additional tests administered by any qualified person of his choosing.

8.    7 A.L.R.2d 8.  Presumption of gratuity need not apply where adult or emancipated child, by prearrangement with parent, gives up established home and moves into home of parent, not for purpose of reestablishing family relationship, but for purpose of rendering services of an extraordinarily burdensome nature over long period of time.

9.    22 A.L.R.2d 244.  Alien who admitted homosexual practices with 6 women was not of good moral character as the ordinary man or woman sees it.

10.   24 A.L.R.2d 873.  Acts of cruelty occurring after his wife became insane could not be relied upon by husband as ground for divorce.

11.   24 A.L.R.2d 1288.  Where client's mental incompetence was well-known to attorney, it was his duty to insist that she procure independent advice before deeding her home to him, and his failure to do so rendered the deed void.

12.   25 A.L.R.2d 315.  Discharge of waitresses who walked off job in protest against discharge of friendly supervisor was not unfair labor practice.

13.   27 A.L.R.2d 498.  Congress never intended dependency exemption to be construed so literally as to allow exemption for

individual whom taxpayer maintains in an illicit relationship in violation of criminal law of state.

14. 37 A.L.R.2d 551. Cost of trip to Lourdes shrine in hope of physical improvement not deductible as medical expense.

15. 91 A.L.R.2d 1120. Claim that juror stated that decision was based upon racial prejudice because defendant was Negro and "that all those people had Cadillacs" was not ground for new trial where there was no showing that any statement by a juror as to race influenced any other juror.

## ASSIGNMENT 7

## A.L.R. BLUE BOOK OF SUPPLEMENTAL DECISIONS:
## USE OF THE A.L.R. BLUE BOOK OF SUPPLEMENTAL DECISIONS
## TO LOCATE LATER DECISIONS AND ANNOTATIONS
## SUPPLEMENTING OR SUPERSEDING ANNOTATIONS PUBLISHED
## IN A.L.R. FIRST SERIES

**Method:**

Refer to the *A.L.R. Blue Book of Supplemental Decisions* bound volumes 1-5 only. Give the full case name and citation according to the latest edition of *The Bluebook* of the *first* case appearing there subsequent to the publication of each of the following annotations (one case only). Cite all supplementing annotations and any superseding annotation.

**Example:**

QUESTION:        83 A.L.R. 127.
ANSWER:          *Davis v. Mississippi,* 394 U.S. 721 (1969).
                 Division III superseded 46 A.L.R.3d 900.

**Questions:**

1.   3 A.L.R. 1682.

2.   56 A.L.R. 666.

3.   23 A.L.R. 1402.

4.   46 A.L.R. 792.

5.   79 A.L.R. 688.

6.   100 A.L.R. 814.

7.   109 A.L.R. 892.

8.   109 A.L.R. 1148.

9.   133 A.L.R. 11.

10.  70 A.L.R. 817.

11.  10 A.L.R. 1137.

12.  58 A.L.R. 737.

13.    66 A.L.R. 439.

14.    77 A.L.R. 1165.

15.    78 A.L.R. 766.

## ASSIGNMENT 8

## POCKET SUPPLEMENTS:
## USE OF A.L.R.3d POCKET SUPPLEMENTS TO LOCATE RELEVANT
## DECISIONS SUBSEQUENT TO ANNOTATIONS PUBLISHED IN
## A.L.R.3d

**Method:**

Refer to the pocket part in the appropriate volume of *A.L.R.3d* for each of the following annotations. Give the name and citation, according to the latest edition of *The Bluebook* of the described subsequent case. You may have to refer to the actual case in order to obtain necessary information for the complete citation. If this Annotation has been superseded indicate the Annotation.

**Example:**

QUESTION:        92 A.L.R.3d 545. Testimony as to assault by defendant upon woman occurring 75 feet from where body of victim in homicide prosecution was found, in remote area, was properly admitted against defendant, even though assault occurred two years after homicide.

ANSWER:          *State v. Ellis*, 208 Neb. 379, 303 N.W.2d 741 (1981).

**Questions:**

1.     11 A.L.R.3d 907. Where an attorney living in one state gave legal advice to his sister living in another state in which he was not admitted, recovery in suit for fee was not barred.

2.     3 A.L.R.3d 829. Law school expenses incurred by taxpayer to maintain and improve skills as forensic pathologist held deductible.

3.     1 A.L.R.3d 844. Calling rabbi a "crook" was not actionable per se.

4.    14 A.L.R.3d 1201. High school student's suspension for wearing Confederate flag on jacket did not violate First and Fourteenth Amendments.

5.    14 A.L.R.3d 993. Promoter of wrestling match held not liable for injuries to patron from being inadvertently bumped by policeman while expelling another patron.

6.    6 A.L.R.3d 1446. Attorney who split legal fees for referrals from person supposedly a member of the bar in Cuba, but not a member of bar in any state in the U.S., was in violation of Code of Professional Responsibility.

7.    21 A.L.R.3d 116. In prosecution for murder by running over deceased with automobile, conviction was sustained where evidence showed that accused intended to kill two other persons at time of act, although there was little or no evidence that he intended to kill the deceased.

8.    21 A.L.R.3d 603. Owner of wild animal (a chimpanzee) was liable to one injured by animal under strict or absolute liability doctrine.

9    21 A.L.R.3d 641. Operating boarding house for mentally retarded persons for financial consideration as violation of covenant restricting use to residential purposes.

10.    27 A.L.R.3d 1274. Surgeon's action in performing operation upon wrong person, while admittedly negligent, did not warrant award of punitive damages where surgeon did not know that he was operating upon wrong patient.

11.    27 A.L.R.3d 794. If one who was beneficiary under insurance policies upon lives of his wife and daughter was insane when he killed them, he would be entitled to proceeds.

12.    17 A.L.R.3d 1442. In malpractice action alleging that attorney failed to file personal injury action within the statute of limitations period, expert testimony as to reasonable settlement value or verdict value was inadmissible.

13.    38 A.L.R.3d 419.  Although square dancer might have assumed risks inherent in square dancing, such as being kicked by another dancer, she did not assume risk of faulty and dangerous floor.

14.    40 A.L.R.3d 444.  Word "child" as used in statute means unborn child whose heart is beating, who is experiencing electronically measurable brain waves, who is discernibly moving, and who is so far developed as to be capable of surviving trauma of birth with aid of usual medical facilities.

# ASSIGNMENT 9

## POCKET SUPPLEMENTS:
## USE OF POCKET SUPPLEMENTS (POCKET PARTS) TO A.L.R.3d, A.L.R. 4th, AND A.L.R. Fed. TO LOCATE LATER CASES THAT SUPPLEMENT THE ANNOTATION.

**Method:**

Refer to the pocket supplement of the appropriate volume of *A.L.R.3d*, *A.L.R.4th* or *A.L.R. Federal* and provide the name of the *first* case that supplements the *A.L.R.* volume and section number in the following problems.

**Example:**

| | |
|---|---|
| QUESTION: | 2 A.L.R. Fed. 18 §9(a) |
| ANSWER: | *Andrews v. Maher* |

**Questions:**

1.  2 A.L.R. Fed. 376

2.  1 A.L.R.4th 411§2(b)

3.  74 A.L.R.4th 32 §17

4.  2 A.L.R.4th 27 §8(g)

5.  13 A.L.R. Fed. 145 §2(b)

6.  8 A.L.R.4th 70 §2(b)

7.  14 A.L.R.4th 227 §23(b)

8.  13 A.L.R.4th 52 §5

9.  44 A.L.R.4th 271 §4(b)

10.  20 A.L.R.4th 23 §7

11.  18 A.L.R.4th 249 §7

12.     23 A.L.R. Fed. 895 §4(a)

13.     15 A.L.R.4th 294 §6(a)

14.     4 A.L.R. Fed. 123 §18(a)

15.     43 A.L.R.4th 410 §38(a)

# ASSIGNMENT 10

# THEME AND DRILL PROBLEMS

**Theme Problem I:**

A.    Using the *ALR Index* and *A.L.R.* volumes, answer the following:

    1.    Give the title and citation of an *A.L.R.* annotation on the defacto segregation of the races in public schools.

    2.    On what case is the annotation based?

    3.    Where are open enrollment plans discussed?

    4.    Cite a related law review article by Fiss.

    5.    In what section can a California case be found?

    6.    Cite a federal case from Texas that comments on §2(b).

    7.    Has this annotation been superseded or supplemented?

    8.    Where might one look in *Am. Jur. 2d* for a related discussion?

    9.    Where can one find an *A.L.R. 2d* Comment-Note on Racial Segregation?

    10.    Where is *Brown* cited in this annotation?

B.    Using the same volume of *A.L.R. 3d*, answer the following:

    1.    Give the name and citation of an annotation that discusses marriage or pregnancy of a public school student as grounds for expulsion or exclusion, or of restriction of activity.

    2.    In what section is there discussion of situations where exclusion and expulsion have been upheld?

    3.    What earlier annotation does this annotation supersede?

    4.    On what case is this annotation based?

5. Where could one find a related annotation on the application of state law to sex discrimination in sports?

6. Who wrote the briefs of counsel for appellant?

C. Using the same volume, give the citations for the following cases:

1. *McCrossen v. United States*

2. *Yarrington v. Thornburg*

3. *Russell v. Casebolt*

## Theme Problem II:

A. Using the *ALR Index* and A.L.R. volumes, answer the following questions:

1. Give the title and citation of an annotation dealing with the issue of whether a divorced parent's voluntary contribution to a child's education expenses justified the modifications of the spousal support award.

2. What section does the court hold that the voluntary payment of education expenses by the parent paying spousal support justified a reduction in the amount of alimony payments?

3. Has the annotation been superseded or supplemented?

4. Where in *Am. Jur. Trials* is the same topic discussed?

5. In the same volume, find an annotation that discusses an employer's liability to an employee for failure to provide a work environment free from tobacco smoke.

B. Using the annotation found in A.5, answer the following:

1. Where would the suggestion that the lawyer request the court to take judicial notice of scientific evidence supporting the allegation that tobacco smoke has a deleterious effect on nonsmokers, in general, be discussed?

2. Name a case that updates any section of this annotation.

3. Which jurisdictions are represented in this annotation?

4. In which volume is there a discussion of a collection of cases dealing with an employee's right to an injunction to prevent exposure to tobacco smoke in the workplace?

## Drill Problem I:

A. Turn to 69 A.L.R.3d 845 (1976) and answer the following:

1. What sections of this annotation cite Louisiana cases?

2. Where could one find discussion of the incapacity of a plaintiff to sue?

3. Where in Am. Jur. 2d could you find a related discussion?

4. On what case is this annotation based?

5. Are there any new cases on § 6 since the annotation was published?

6. Where could one find a related annotation on the power of a court to vacate or modify an order granting a new trial in a civil case?

B. Locate annotations on the following topics:

1. The validity of traffic regulations requiring motorcyclists to wear protective headgear.

2. The attempt to commit assault as a criminal offense.

3. The liability of Roy Rogers if Trigger kicks someone.

C. Specify any annotations that supplement or supersede any of the following:

1. 25 A.L.R.2d 1077

2. 41 A.L.R. 1437

3.      75 A.L.R.3d 1000

D.      Use the *A.L.R. Blue Books* (Permanent Edition and Supplements) to answer the following:

1.      Cite a case in 379 N.Y.S.2d that updates 90 A.L.R. 101-116.

2.      Is there a 1977 Louisiana decision related to 52 A.L.R. 935-341? If so, give the citation.

E.      Use the *A.L.R.2d Later Case Service* to answer the following:

1.      Cite a case updating 12 A.L.R.2d 524-573, that involves beer barrels.

2.      Cite a Pennsylvania case in 227 Pa. Super. that updates § 26 of 55 A.L.R.2d 554-63A.

F.      Use the pocket parts or supplements of *A.L.R.3d* and *A.L.R. Fed.* to answer the following:

1.      Cite a Connecticut case that updated § 25 of 72 A.L.R.3d 131-329.

2.      Cite an Arizona case that updates § 10 of 67 A.L.R.3d 824-889.

3.      Cite two *Am. Jur. 2d* sections that discuss 31 A.L.R.3d 1448-1454.

## Drill Problem II:

A.      Turn to 84 A.L.R.3d 665 and answer the following:

1.      Where in this annotation can one find discussion of the waiving of a guardian's consent?

2.      Where in *Am. Jur. 2d* could one find a discussion of the same topic?

3.      Where are any Oklahoma cases cited?

4.     Where could one find related discussion on the adoption of an adult?

5.     On what case is this annotation based?

B.     Locate annotations on the following topics:

1.     Statutes related to sexual psychopaths.

2.     Exemption from taxation of a municipally owned auditorium.

3.     The application of zoning ordinances to a research laboratory.

C.     Specify any annotations that supplement or supersede any of the following:

1.     163 A.L.R. 1188

2.     153 A.L.R. 329

3.     1 A.L.R. 148

D.     Use the *A.L.R. Blue Books* (Permanent Edition and Supplements) to answer the following:

1.     Cite a case in 324 N.E.2d that cites to the annotation at 10 A.L.R. 1591-1594.

2.     What is the latest information on 15 A.L.R. 125-145?

E.     Use the *A.L.R.2d Later Case Service* to answer the following:

1.     Cite a Conn. case updating §3 of 15 A.L.R.2d 11-94.

2.     Cite a Utah case that updates §39(b) of 70 A.L.R.2d 268-335.

F.     Use the pocket parts of *A.L.R.3d* and *A.L.R. Fed.* to answer the following:

1.     Cite a 5th Circuit case from Texas that updates §3 of 14 A.L.R. Fed. 806-818.

2.      Cite an Am. Jur. Proof of Facts 2d article on 60 A.L.R.3d, 880-923.

3.      Cite a 6th Circuit decision updating §6, 3 A.L.R. Fed. 569-586.

# Chapter 18

# LEGAL PERIODICALS AND INDEXES

## ASSIGNMENT 1

### AUTHOR INDEX PROBLEMS -- INDEX TO LEGAL PERIODICALS, CURRENT LAW INDEX, LEGALTRAC

PART I.        Using *Index to Legal Periodicals,* locate and cite the following:

**Questions:**

1.      R.H. Freilich, Missouri law of land use controls.

2.      R.A. Jensen, Effect of federal truth in lending act.

3.      L.F. Powell, Jr., Contributory negligence.

4.      J.O. Newman, Prosecutor and defender reform.

5.      R.B. Ginsburg, Gender and the Constitution.

6.      W.H. Pedrick, War measures and contract liability.

7.      W.H. Rehnquist, Subdivision trusts and the bankruptcy act.

8.      I. Younger, Congressional investigations and executive secrecy.

9.      K.N. Llewellyn, Lecture on appellate advocacy.

10.     S. Mentschikoff, Commercial arbitration.

11.     J.B. Fordham, Home rule powers in theory and practice.

12.     J. O'Connell, Public opinion on no-fault auto insurance.

13.     S.T. Agnew, Case for revenue sharing.

14.     T.F. Eagleton, Congress and the war powers.

15.    R.E. Keeton, No-fault insurance: a status report.

16.    R.F. Kennedy, Halfway houses pay off.


PART II.    Using *Current Law Index,* locate and cite the following:

**Questions:**

1.    Paul Verkuil, Judicial review of informal rulemaking.

2.    Aviam Soifer, Complacency and Constitutional law.

3.    Albert Borowitz, Harvard murder case.

4.    William Epstein, Dialectics and American legal education.

5.    Robert Gorman, Recording musician and union power.

6.    Sylvia Law, Sex and the Constitution.

7.    Gerald Frug, Ideology of bureaucracy in American law.

8.    Monroe Price, Text and intellect.

9.    Leonard Levy, Origins of free press clause.

10.    Abner Mikva, Footnotes.


PART III.    Using LegalTrac, locate and cite the following:

**Questions:**

1.    Ralph S. Brown, Eligibility for copyright protection.

2.    Robert Bennett, Judges and original intent.

3.    Roberto Ungar, The Critical Legal Studies movement.

4.    Gerald Korngold, Privately held conservation servitudes.

5.    Michael Tigar, Mail fraud.

6.      Lawrence Tribe, Jurisdictional gerrymandering.

7.      Fred R. Shapiro, Most-cited law review articles.

8.      Francis X. Beytaug, Privacy in perspective.

9.      John Hart Ely, Business law vs. public interest law.

10.     Mark G. Yudof, Effective schools and federal and state constitutions.

11.     Lily Fu, use of prior, uncounseled misdemeanors.

12.     Dee Wampler, sentencing.

13.     Kenneth Clevenger, Cross-examination.

14.     Stephen Younger, ADR proceedings.

# ASSIGNMENT 2

# CASE APPROACH TO PERIODICAL ARTICLES

PART I.   Using the *Index to Legal* Periodicals, locate and cite the first (by date of law review issue) student comment on the following cases:

1.   *In Re Permian Basin Area Rate Cases,* 88 S. Ct. 1344 (1968).

2.   *People v. McKinnon,* 7 Cal. 3d 889, 500 P.2d 1097 (1972).

3.   *Nathan Cummings,* 61 T.C. 1 (1973).

4.   *Office of Communication of the United Church of Christ v. FCC.*

5.   *Investors Management Co., SEC Exchange Act Release no. 9267,* CCH Fed. Sec. L. Rep. para. 78, 163 (1971).

6.   *Hopkins v. Gardner,* 374 F.2d 726.

7.   *U.S. v. 16179 Molso Italian .22 Caliber Winlee Derringer Convertible Starter Guns,* 433 F.2d 463.

8.   *Brasserie de Haecht v. Wilkin-Janssen,* Case 43/72 C.M.L.R. 287 (1973).

9.   *Hicks v. Hicks,* 155 S.E.2d 799.

10.   *Davis v. Thornton,* 180 N.W.2d 11.

11.   *DeFunis v. Odegaard,* No. 741727 (Washington Superior Court for King County, Sept. 22, 1971).

12.   *FTC v. B.F. Goodrich Co.,* 242 F.2d 31.

13.   *Lorenz v. State.* 406 P.2d 278.

14.   *Communist Party of the U.S. v. Catherwood,* 81 S. Ct. 1465.

15.   *Hialeah Race Course, Inc. v. Gulfstream Park Racing Association, Inc.,* 37 So.2d 692.

16. *Tuscarora Indian Nation v. FPC*, 265 F.2d 338.

17. *Hoffa v. U.S.*, 87 S. Ct. 408.

18. *Alden-Rochelle, Inc. v. American Society of Composers, Authors and Publishers*, 80 F. Supp. 888.

19. *City of Mangum v. Brownlee*, 75 P.2d 174.

20. *Award of Her Majesty Queen Elizabeth II for the Arbitration of a Controversy Between the Argentine Republic and the Republic of Chile Concerning Certain Parts of the Boundary Between their Territories*, Court of Arbitration, November 21, 1966.

21. *Pierre V. Administrator*, 553 So. 2d 442

22. *Baesler v. Continental Grain Company*, 900 F.2d 1193.

23. *Barnes v. Glen Theatre, Inc.*, 111 S. Ct. 2456 (1991).

24. *Colorado v. Idarado Mining Co.*, 916 F.2d 1486 (1990).

25. *California Fed. Sav. & Loan Ass'n. v. Guerra*, 107 S. Ct. 683.

26. *In re Newhauser*, 579 So. 2d 437.


PART II.   Using *Current Law Index*, locate and give the citation for a periodical article for each of the following cases:

**Questions:**

1. *The Desping R*, (1979) 1 Lloyds Rep. 1 (H.L.).

2. *State ex rel. McCamic v. McCoy*, 276 S.E.2d 534 (1981).

3. *City of Berkeley v. Superior Court*, 606 P. 2d 362 (1980).

4. *St. Martin Evangelical Lutheran Church v. South Dakota*, 101 S. Ct. 2142 (1981).

5. *In re Doe*, 440 A.2d 712 (1982).

6.     *People v. Bustamante,* 634 P.2d 927 (1981).

7.     *MBL (USA) Corp. v. Diekman,* 445 N.E.2d 418 (1983).

8.     *In re Estate of Bartlett,* 680 P.2d 369 (1984).

9.     *Watt v. California,* 104 S. Ct. 656 (1984).

10.    *Colombia v. Peru,* 1950 I.C.J. *266.*

11.    *Braschi v. Stohl Ass. Co.,* 543 N.E.2d 49 (1989).

12.    *State v. Sherlock,* 768 P.2d 1290 (1989).

13.    *Cross v. American Country Insurance Co.,* 875 F.2d 625 (1989).

14.    *In re Green,* 73 B.R. 893 (1987).

15.    *City of Renton v. Playtime Theatres,* 106 S. Ct. 925 (1986).

16.    *Roberts v. Dunbar Funeral Home,* 339 S.E.2d 517 (1986)


PART III.     Using LegalTrac, locate and give the citation for a periodical article for each of the following cases:

**Questions:**

1.     *John A. Hall Construction Co. v. Boone & Darr, Inc.,* 302 N.W.2d 850 (1981).

2.     *City of Auburn v. Mavis,* 468 N.E.2d 584 (1984).

3.     *In re IBM,* 687 F.2d 591 (1982).

4.     *R. v. Adams* (1980) All E.R. 473.

5.     *St. Alexius Hospital v. Eckert,* 284 N.W.2d 441 (1979).

6.     *In re Marriage of Allen,* 626 P.2d 16 (1981).

7.     *Estate of Bahen v. United States,* 305 F.2d 827 (1962).

8. *Tiffany Fine Arts Inc. v. United States,* No. 83-1007 (U.S. Jan. 9, 1985).

9. *McKay v.* Davis, 653 P.2d 860 (1982).

10. *Bailey Estate v. Commissioner,* 81 T.C. 246 (1983).

11. *Brown Bag Software v. Synantec Corp.*, 960 F.2d 1465 (9th Cir. 1992).

12. *American Trucking Assn's v. Smith,* 58 U.S.L.W. 4704 (1990.

13. *Jones Brothers Construction v. Riley,* 556 N.E. 2d 602 (1990).

14. *Anderson Chemical v. Portals Water Treatment,* 768 F. Supp. 1568 (1991).

**ASSIGNMENT 3**

**PROBLEM APPROACH TO THE INDEX TO FINDING PERIODICAL ARTICLES**

PART I.        Using *Index to Legal Periodicals,* answer the following:

**Questions:**

1.        Find a 1966 article concerned with attitudes toward the Los Angeles race riot.

2.        Locate a case involving a prisoner's rights under the Federal Tort Claims Act, and a 1955 law review comment thereon.

3.        Find a 1973 discussion of insuring the condominium.

4.        Find a 1971 article on the rule against perpetuities and the spendthrift trust in New York.

5.        Cite a 1960 note on the common law liability of liquor vendors.

6.        Find a 1973 article concerned with discrimination against women in the extension of credit.

7.        Locate a 1967 article on blood transfusions where an adult Jehovah's Witness is involved.

8.        Locate a 1969 note calling for legislation to protect computer programs.

9.        Cite a 1955 and 1956 article (printed two places) concerned with the fingerprinting of bar applicants.

10.        Cite a 1968 model movie censorship ordinance.

11.        Find a 1974 article concerned with airline "bumping" and baggage loss.

12. Cite a 1952 article concerned with the U.S. General Accounting Office's right to inspect government contractors' records.

13. Find a 1966 article on the malpractice of psychiatrists.

14. Locate an article discussing a (1959) case involving negligence for animals on the highway as a cause of a motor vehicle accident.

15. Find a survey of the work of the U.S. Court of Appeals for the Sixth Circuit for the year 1971- 72.

16. Locate a 1955 article on the drafting of a book publishing contract.

17. Find a 1957 article concerned with the origin of credit life insurance.

18. Cite a 1971 article on computer program protection.

19. Find a 1975 article dealing with live organ transplants from minor donors in Massachusetts.

20. Cite a 1967 article discussing slumlordism as a tort.

21. Locate an article on battered women who kill.

22. Cite a 1991 article on the limited liability company.

23. Find a 1992 article on insurance coverage and therapist-patient sexual relations.

24. Cite a 1991 article on ethical considerations for music industry professionals.

25. Locate an article on fraudulent conveyances and the Bankruptcy Code.

26. Cite a 1992 article providing international adjudication of arbitrary conduct.

PART II.     Using *Current Law Index,* answer the following:

**Questions:**

1.     Cite a 1980 article on tax collection policies and practices.

2.     Locate a 1981 article on rethinking rent control in New Jersey.

3.     Find a 1982 article on community property taxation and joint and several federal income tax liability.

4.     Locate an article from 1983 discussing federal injunctions and the public interest.

5.     Find a 1984 article on whether automated tellers at groceries constitute branch banking.

6.     Find a 1984 article about the role of religion in the public school curriculum.

7.     Cite a 1985 article suggesting tort damages for fear and risk of injury.

8.     Locate a 1985 article on modifying U.S. acceptance of the compulsory jurisdiction of the World Court.

9.     Find a 1985 speech on the private management of asbestos litigation.

10.     Cite a 1985 discussion of taking voting rights seriously.

11.     Locate a 1990 article updating medical negligence.

12.     Find a 1990 article on the motorcycle helmet defense.

13.     Cite a 1988 article on the coke habit.

14.     Locate a 1988 article on entrapment as a defense.

15.     Cite a 1988 article on child sexual abuse evaluations.

PART III        Using LegalTrac, answer the following:

**Questions:**

1.      Cite a 1983 discussion of the use and abuse of liquidated damages in federal defense contracts.

2.      Locate a 1986 bibliography on gun control.

3.      Find a 1986 article about AIDS in the workplace.

4.      Cite a 1984 article explaining resolving civil disputes in a church environment.

5.      Find a 1985 article which gives the English perspective on the American abortion debate.

6.      Locate a 1984 discussion of commercial paper as "security" under the Glass-Steagall Act.

7.      Locate a 1986 article explaining New York's new rules for handling asbestos.

8.      Find a 1985 article on job burnout among narcotics investigators.

9.      Find a 1986 article on the role of in-vitro fertilization in the treatment of infertility.

10.     Cite a 1986 explanation of why the Treasury dropped its 20-year bonds.

11.     Locate a 1993 article on the abortion rights of minors.

12.     Find a 1994 article on gun control in Hollywood.

13.     Cite a 1994 article on the rise in health care insurance premiums.

# Chapter 19

# TREATISES, RESTATEMENTS, UNIFORM LAWS, AND MODEL ACTS

## ASSIGNMENT 1

## USE OF TORTS TREATISES

**Method:**

    (1)    Answer each problem with either a "Yes" or "No" according to the majority view.

    (2)    Using the source indicated in parentheses find the answers to the following questions. Properly cite the applicable section number and page. For example:

        F. Harper & F. James, Jr., & O. Gray *The Law of Torts* sec. _, at _ (3d ed. 2006).
        *Prosser and Keeton on the Law of Torts* sec. _, at _ (5th ed. 1984).

    (3)    Properly cite the cases or other materials as requested.

**Questions:**

    1.    Can loud noises constitute an actionable private nuisance? Cite a law review article on point cited in a footnote. (Prosser & Keeton)

    2.    May a woman bring an action in battery for being kissed without her consent? Cite a Missouri case on point. (Harper, James & Gray)

    3.    Does a person have a right to dynamite a house if this is necessary to stop the spread of a conflagration that threatens a town? Cite a California case on point. (Prosser and Keeton)

4.  May a child maintain an action for the consequences of prenatal injuries? Cite a 1951 New York case on point. (Harper, James & Gray)

5.  Is it necessary for a person to be physically restrained in order to bring an action for false imprisonment? Cite a 1924 Maryland case on point. (Prosser and Keeton)

6.  If, without negligence, a person cuts down a tree on his own land and it falls on adjoining land, does the adjoining landowner have a cause of action? Cite an 1841 North Carolina case on point. (Prosser and Keeton)

7.  Does an experienced baseball spectator have a cause of action if he is injured by a batted ball while attending a baseball game? Cite a Washington case on point. (Harper, James & Gray)

8.  Is "hostile intent" the gist of an action of battery? (Prosser and Keeton)

9.  May damages be awarded for mental distress suffered at the hands of a practical joker? Cite an English case on point. (Harper, James & Gray)

10. May an insane person be held liable for wrongful death? Cite a 1887 case on point. (Prosser and Keeton)

11. May a father be held liable for the damage caused by his son's negligent driving of the family car? Cite a 1915 Georgia case on point. (Harper, James & Gray)

12. May a funeral parlor located in a residential community be considered a private nuisance? Cite a Michigan case holding that a nuisance exists. (Prosser and Keeton)

13. Can a defendant who engages in blasting activities within city limits be held strictly liable for concussion damages? Cite a 1963 Indiana case on point. (Prosser and Keeton)

14. Should a minor engaged in driving an automobile be held to the same standard of care as an adult? Cite a 1981 Minnesota case on point. (Prosser and Keeton)

15. Does the erroneous dissemination of a credit rating by a credit rating bureau, falsely alleging an account was overdue, constitute defamation? Cite a 1918 Florida case on point. (Harper & James)

16. Are police and firemen deemed invites rather than licensees when summoned to a public place in the line of duty? Cite a 1974 Nebraska case on point relating to police.(Prosser and Keeton)

17. Is an insane person held to the same standard of conduct as that required of a sane person? Cite a 1905 law review article on point. (Prosser and Keeton)

18. Does a municipality enjoy the same sovereign immunity as the state? Cite the original 1788 case on point. (Harper & James)

19. Is an ordinary man free to act in reliance upon the opinion of an expert jeweler as to the value of a diamond? Cite a 1862 Michigan case a point. (Prosser and Keeton)

20. Does the physician's standard of conduct differ from that of the reasonable man in general? Cite a 1959 law review article. (Prosser and Keeton)

21. In a civil action for damages against more than one person, are all of the defendants who acted in concert equally liable? Cite a 1920 Minnesota case on point. (Prosser and Keeton)

22. Is owner of a known vicious watchdog liable for damages if the dog attacks a trespasser who has not been warned of the dog's presence? Cite a 1837 New York case on point. (Harper, James & O. Gray).

23. Is a credit agency, such as a mutual credit organization, liable for defamation of character of a person as a bad credit risk if made in good faith? Cite a 1959 California case on point. (Prosser and Keeton)

24. Has there been a false arrest where a woman's purse was taken from her as security so that she would not leave a store? Cite a 1946 Kentucky case on point. (Prosser and Keeton)

25. Is the owner of a leopard responsible for injury it may cause? Cite a 1919 California case on point. (Harper, James & Gray)

26.    Is it considered trespass to mine under adjoining land? Cite a 1863 California case on point. (Harper, James & Gray).

27.    Does an automobile manufacturer give an implied warranty as to the safety of his product? Cite the leading 1960 case and the classic periodical article which traced subsequent development of the principle. (Prosser and Keeton)

28.    Is snatching a newspaper out of another person's hand sufficient to satisfy the elements of battery? Cite an Illinois case on point. (Harper, James & Gray).

29.    Is a person in charge of a restaurant privileged to retain for thirty minutes a customer he suspects may not have paid his bill? Cite an 1873 Massachusetts case on point.(Harper, James & Gray).

30.    Is a child liable for torts such as slander of defamation of another? Cite a 1898 Missouri case on point. (Harper, James & Gray)

# ASSIGNMENT 2

## USE OF A.L.I. RESTATEMENTS

**Method:**

(1)     Answer each problem with either a "Yes" or "No".

(2)     Refer to the *Restatement (Second) of Property* or the *Restatement (Second) of Torts* (1965) or the *Restatement (Second) of Contracts* (1981), and give the applicable section number of the restatement volume where the answer was found. (Do not consult appendices or pocket parts).

(3)     Cite case on point if question requires this information.

**Questions:**

A.     *Restatement (Second) of Property* .

    1.     Is an oral modification of a valid lease invalid if both the original and remaining periods exceed the period specified in the controlling statute of frauds?

    2.     Do all states have statutes which prohibit landlords from refusing to lease to an individual on the basis of sex?

    3.     When a donor of property describes the beneficiaries thereof as the "children" of a designated person, are children born out of wedlock excluded?

    4.     Can a donor include a provision designed to prevent the acquisition of property on account of rejection of certain religious beliefs.

    5.     Are noncompetitive clauses illegal in a rental agreement:

B.     *Restatement (Second) of Torts.*

    1.     Will contributory negligence bar recovery in a suit based upon an intentionally inflicted tort?  Cite a 1963 Alaska case on point.

    2.     Can a threat made merely in words constitute an assault?  Cite a 1960 Pennsylvania case on point.

3. Is a soldier liable civilly for injury to another which results from following the orders of a superior court? Cite a 1941 Massachusetts case on point.

4. Will the courts recognize a citizen arrest without a warrant where the citizen-passerby is a witness to the crime which has been committed? Cite a Pennsylvania case on point.

5. Does the granting of permission by a homeowner to a canvasser to enter a home make such canvasser an invitee as opposed to a licensee? Cite a 1919 Washington case on point?

6. Does the so-called "reasonable man" standard apply equally to children? Cite a 1934 Connecticut case on point.

7. Is an actor liable for negligent conduct which results in emotional disturbance alone, without bodily harm or other compensable damage? Cite the first A.L.R. annotation listed under this section as a cross reference.

C. *Restatement (Second) of Contracts.*

1. Is a promise in a restraint of trade situation a relevant contractual issue?

2. When one of two promisors of the same performance in a contract dies, is the estate of the deceased provision relieved of the contractual obligation? Is there a 1986 case on point?

3. Is an acceptance under an option contract operative only after reciept by the offeror? Is there a 1988 case on this issue?

4. Within the Statute of Frauds, is a promise to marry ever valid consideration? Is there a 1990 case on this issue?

5. Are punitive damages ever recoverable for a breach of contract when a tort has also occurred? Is there a 1990 Pennsylvania case on this issue.

# ASSIGNMENT 3

# DRILL PROBLEMS AND THEME PROBLEMS

## Drill Problem I:

A.      Using J. Calamari & J. Perillo, *The Law of Contracts* (5th ed. 2003), answer the following, citing the supporting section and/or case where applicable.

      1.      Does a sealed contract require  consideration?

      2.      Where can one find a discussion of *Redgrave v. Boston Symphony* Orchestra?

B       Using *Prosser and Keeton on The Law of Torts* (5th ed. 1984), answer the following, citing a supporting section or page where appropriate.

      1.      Can a child recover for damages due to an injury caused to the mother when pregnant?

      2.      Have lunatics generally been held liable for their torts?

## Drill Problem II:

A.      Using J. Calamari & J Perillo, *The Law of Contracts* (5th ed. 2003), answer the following, citing the supporting section and/or case where applicable:

      1.      What is the modern definition of duress?

      2.      Cite a case where an unlicensed milk dealer was allowed to recover despite the fact the services rendered were illegal.

B.      Using *Prosser and Keeton on The Law of Torts* (5th ed. 1984), answer the following, citing a supporting section or page where appropriate.

      1.      Does an action lie against a dealer who describes what turns out to be a lemon as a "dandy," a "bearcat" and a "sweet job"? Cite a 1932 Texas case.

      2.      Where can one find discussion of *Clary v. Hale*?

3.      Does the consent of the plaintiff constitute an absolute privilege to speak without fear of being sued for defamation?

## Drill Problem III:

A.      Using J. Calamari & J. Perillo, *The Law of Contracts* (5th ed. 2003), answer the following, citing the supporting section and/or case where applicable.

1.      Will a plaintiff be granted the equitable relief of specific performance if he comes to court with "unclean" hands?

2.      Where can one find mention of *Dallas Cowboys Football Club v. Harris*?

B.      Using *Prosser and Keeton on The Law of Torts* (5th ed. 1984), answer the following, citing a supporting section or page where appropriate.

1.      At common law could the wife sue for interference with domestic relations?

2.      When did the special rule as to injuries to children who are hurt while trespassing first appear in the United States?

3.      Does revenge qualify as a defense to intentional assault?

## Theme Problem

A.      *Roe v. Wade* dealt with constitutional issues of privacy. Using L. Tribe, *American Constitutional Law* (3d ed. 2000), answer the following. Put your answers in *The Bluebook* form.

1.      List the first three places that *Roe v. Wade* is discussed.

2.      Who was the first President to invoke executive privilege?

3.      On what date was the Equal Rights Amendment passed by Congress? Where does the text of the amendment appear?

B.      Using J. Nowak, R. Rotunda & J. Young, *Constitutional Law* (7th edition, 2004), answer the following.

1.      Give the first two places that *Roe v. Wade* is discussed.

2.      May a state eliminate the teaching of certain ideas because they conflict with certain religious beliefs?

3.      What Edmund Wilson novel was adjudged obscene?

# Chapter 21

# INTERNATIONAL LAW

## ASSIGNMENT 1

### PRE-1950 UNITED STATES TREATIES AND INTERNATIONAL AGREEMENTS

**Sources**:    *Treaties in Force*, 2007,
http://www.state.gov/s/l/treaty/treaties/2007/indexhtml

*Treaties and Other International Agreements of the
United States of America, 1776-1949*, by Charles E.
Bevans;

*United States Treaties and Other International
Agreements Cumulative Index, 1776-1949*, compiled by
Igor I. Kavass and Mark A. Michael; and

*Shepard's Federal Statute Citations*, for part 5 of each
question.

**Method:**

Give the following for each treaty or international agreement listed
below:

(1)    Its citation in *Statutes at Large* and concurrent citation in Bevans'
Treaties (if any), for example, 43 Stat. 1621, 6 Bevans 1033;

(2)    Its date or dates of signature, opening for signature, exchange of
notes, etc. (but not the dates of ratification, proclamation, or entry
into force), for example, Nov. 10, 1922; and

(3)    Its E.A.S., T.S., or T.I.A.S. number, for example, T.S. No.
668.

(4)    Is it in force?  If so, give the date of its entry into force.  Also
give year and page reference to the 2007 edition of *Treaties in
Force* containing this information, for example, April 27, 1923,
2007 T.I.F. 36.

(5)     Its subsequent judicial, legislative, or diplomatic developments
(if any), as shown in *Shepard's Federal Statute Citations 1996*.
Copy as appearing in Shepard's, for example, 290US294,
78LE324, 54SC105.

The easiest way to determine the answer to questions (1), (2), (3), and (4)
is to first check *Treaties in Force*. If you do not find the answer in *Treaties in
Force*, check the index to the Bevans' work or the Kavass, Michael Index.

*Treaties in Force*, though not the best index ever produced, is easy to
use. It has two main divisions; Part 1 for bilateral treaties and agreements
between the United States and other countries or political entities and Part 2 for
multilateral treaties and agreements. Part 1 is arranged alphabetically by
country, with subject entries under each country. Territories of a country are
placed at the end of that country. Part 2 is arranged alphabetically by subject.

The weakness of *Treaties in Force* is the choice and number of subject
headings and the inadequate use of cross references. However, once you
determine if the treaty or agreement is bilateral or multilateral, you can usually
find the answer. If bilateral and you know the country, you can quickly scan the
appropriate or related subject headings under the country in Part 1 and determine
whether the treaty or agreement is in force. If the treaty or agreement is
multilateral, you can determine whether it is in force by scanning the appropriate
correlated subject headings in Part 2.

If the treaty or agreement is not listed in *Treaties in Force*, the quickest
way to find it is to search the index volume to Bevans' work. This will lead you
directly to the answer. You can also search the Kavass, Michael Cumulative
Index. The advantage of the former is that it leads you directly to the text in the
appropriate Bevans' volume.

You can answer question (5) by Shepardizing the citation in *Shepard's
Federal Statute Citations*.

## Questions and Answers:

1.  QUESTION:     Commerce and Navigation Treaty with
                  Turkey

2.  QUESTION:     Treaty of Arbitration with Estonia, 1930

3.  QUESTION:     Agreement with Canada to raise the level
                  of Lake St. Francis

4.  QUESTION:     Parcel post agreement with Bahamas, 1936

5.    QUESTION:        Treaty establishing friendly relations with
                       Hungary, 1921

6.    QUESTION:        Agreement with Norway relating to
                       customs treatment of importations for
                       consular offices

7.    QUESTION:        Agreement with Sweden for exemption of
                       pleasure yachts from navigation dues.

8.    QUESTION:        Provisional agreement about commerce
                       with Egypt

9.    QUESTION:        Treaty of arbitration with Sweden

10.   QUESTION:        Treaty about traveling salesmen with
                       Venezuela

11.   QUESTION:        Aviation treaty relating to pilot licenses to
                       operate civil aircraft within Sri Lanka.

12.   QUESTION:        Fuel and vegetable oil agreement with
                       Argentina

13.   QUESTION:        Exchange of official publications with
                       Brazil

14.   QUESTION:        Agreement relative to postal money orders
                       in Postal Union of the Americas and Spain,
                       1936

15.   QUESTION:        Agricultural experiment station agreement
                       with Ecuador, 1942

16.   QUESTION:        Military obligations agreement with
                       Finland

17.   QUESTION:        Agreement for "Haitinization" with Haiti

18.   QUESTION:        Rights of U.S. in Iraq

19.   QUESTION:        Agreement for maritime claims and
                       litigation with France

# ASSIGNMENT 2

## POST-1950 UNITED STATES TREATIES AND INTERNATIONAL AGREEMENTS

**Sources:**    *Treaties in Force*, 2007,
http://www.state.gov/s/l/treaty/treaties/2007/index.htm.

Cumulative Index to *United States Treaties and Other International Agreements, 1950-1970,* compiled by Igor I. Kavass and Adolf Sprudzs; and

*Shepard's Federal Statute Citations, 1996,* for Part (5) of each question.

## Method:

Give the following for each treaty or international agreement listed below:

(1)    Its citation in *United States Treaties and Other International Agreements*, for example, 12 U.S.T. 908;

(2)    Its date or dates of signature, opening for signature, exchange of notes, etc. (but not the dates of ratification, proclamation, or entry into (force), for example, Oct. 1, 1951; and

(3)    Its T.I.A.S. number, for example, T.I.A.S. No. 4797.

(4)    Is it in force?  If so, the date of its entry into force.  Also give year and page references to the 2007 edition of *Treaties in Force* containing this information, for example, July 30, 1961, 2007 T.I.F. 40.

(5)    Its subsequent judicial, legislative, or diplomatic developments (if any), as shown in *Shepard's  Statute Edition, 1996*.  Copy as appearing in Shepard's, for example, 297FS349.

The easiest way to determine the answer to questions (1), (2), (3), and (4) is to first check *Treaties in Force*.  (See the explanation for the use of *Treaties in Force* under Assignment 1.)  If you do not find the answer in *Treaties in Force*, check the appropriate volume of the Kavass and Sprudzs work.  Volumes 3,

Country, and 4, Subject, will, in most cases, supply the answer if *Treaties in Force* does not.

You can answer question (5) by Shepardizing the citation in *Shepard's Federal Statute Citations, 1996.*

**Questions and Answers:**

1. QUESTION: Economic cooperation agreement with France, 1950 amendment

2. QUESTION: Economic cooperation agreement with Italy, 1950 amendment

3. QUESTION: U.S. Educational Commission agreement with Korea, 1950

4. QUESTION: Agreement with United Kingdom concerning civil airport facilities in Bermuda, 1951

5. QUESTION: Agreement concerning administration of income tax in Canada of U.S. Government employees in Canada

6. QUESTION: Agreement with Korea concerning mutual security assurances

7. QUESTION: Agreement with Thailand concerning the U.S. Educational Foundation, 1953

8. QUESTION: Agreement with Brazil for a military advisory mission, 1952

9. QUESTION: Agreement with Italy concerning surplus agricultural commodities, March, 1957

10. QUESTION: Agreement with Korea concerning atomic energy cooperation for civil uses, 1958 amendment

11. QUESTION: Agreement with Italy concerning loan of vessel, 1959

12. QUESTION: Double taxation agreement with Argentina concerning the operation of ships and aircraft

13. QUESTION: Agreement concerning participation of Belgian Armed Forces in United Nations Operations in Korea

14. QUESTION: Peace Corps agreement with Bolivia, 1962

15. QUESTION: Convention for the exchange of postal money orders with the colony of British Virginia Islands

# ASSIGNMENT 3

## UNITED NATIONS TREATY SERIES
## (CHRONOLOGICAL INDEX)

**Source:**     *United Nations Treaty Series Cumulative Index,* Nos. 1-11
(covering volumes 1-750 of *United Nations Treaty Series*).

**Method:**

By using the Chronological Index, give the following for each of the
treaties listed below:

(1)     The U.N.T.S. number, e.g. I:7999; and
(2)     The U.N.T.S. volume and page number where the text of the
treaty may be found, e.g. 549 U.N.T.S. 173.

The answers to these problems are relatively easy to find. You have only
to locate the date of the treaty concerned in the Chronological Index of the
appropriate Cumulative Index volumes. You may have to look in several
different volumes, however, to find the date of the treaty or agreement in
question.

**Questions:**

1.     QUESTION:     Charter of the Organization of American
States, April 30, 1948

2.     QUESTION:     Agreement between Italy and the
Netherlands about free assistance before
the courts for indigents and waiver of
security costs, January 9, 1884

3.     QUESTION:     An exchange of notes between Luxemburg
and the Netherlands on freedom of the air
for regular international air services, April
14, 1948

4.     QUESTION:     Agreement between Hungary and Soviet
Union on mutual legal assistance in
matters relating to the temporary presence
of Soviet forces on Hungarian territory,
April 2,1, 1958

5.  QUESTION:   Multipartite agreement for research on the effects of radioactivity in the sea, March 8/10, 1961

6.  QUESTION:   Agreement between Austria and Soviet Union concerning settlement of the technical and commercial questions relating to navigation of the Danube, June 14, 1957

7.  QUESTION:   Loan to Norway by Canada of three frigates, December 20, 1955

8.  QUESTION:   Exchange of notes between Columbia and the United States on the service of nationals of one country in the armed forces of the other, January 27/February 12, 1944

9.  QUESTION:   Multipartite agreement of armistice with Bulgaria, October 28, 1944

10. QUESTION:   General agreement of technical cooperation between Egypt and the United States, May 5, 1951

11. QUESTION:   Trade agreement between India and Burma, September 29, 1951

12. QUESTION:   Agreement for health projects in Korea, September 19, 1951

13. QUESTION:   Commercial agreement between France and Greece, December 23, 1952

14. QUESTION:   Air transport agreement between Luxemburg and Iceland, October 23, 1952

15. QUESTION:   The Brussels Treaty for collaboration in economic, social, and cultural matters, March 17, 1948

16. QUESTION:   Manila accord, July 31, 1963

17.  QUESTION:  Agreement between Canada and France on films and film production, October 11, 1963

18.  QUESTION:  Nordic mutual emergency assistance agreement, October 17, 1963

19.  QUESTION:  Agreement between Netherlands and Nigeria for the development of the Faculty of Engineering at the University of Nigeria, Nsukku, December 4, 1964

20.  QUESTION:  Trade agreement between Australia and Philippines, June 16, 1965

21.  QUESTION:  Consular convention between Finland and Soviet Union, January 24, 1966

22.  QUESTION:  Exchange of notes on the use of seamen's books as travel documents, June 15/20, 1967

23.  QUESTION:  Exchange of notes on abolition of visas between Austria and Dominican Republic, February 21, 1968

24.  QUESTION:  Treaty of friendship between Gabon and Israel, May 15, 1962

25.  QUESTION:  Monetary agreement between Switzerland and the United Kingdom, March 12, 1946

# ASSIGNMENT 4

## UNITED NATIONS TREATY SERIES
## (ALPHABETICAL INDEX)

**Source:** *United Nations Treaty Series Cumulative Index,* Nos. 1-9: (covering volumes 1-650 of *United Nations Treaty Series*).

**Method:**

  By using the Alphabetical Index, give the following for each treaty described below:

  (1) The U.N.T.S. number, e.g. I:7741; and
  (2) The U.N.T.S. volume and page number where the text of the treaty may be found, e.g. 533 U.N.T.S. 157.

  As in the preceding set of questions, the answers to these are relatively easy to find. You have only to locate the correct heading in the Alphabetical Index of the appropriate Cumulative Index volume. The Alphabetical Index has four types of major headings: (1) Countries and Organizations, (2) Subjects,(3) General International Agreements (entered under this heading), and (4) Multipartite Instruments (entered under this heading). All four types are listed in the Alphabetical Index. Most of the answers can be found under the names of the countries in question, but you may have to search in several volumes before finding the answer.

  To make certain that the students cite the answer by using the Alphabetical Index rather than the Chronological Index, you should request that they note the page number of the Cumulative Index where the answer appears. For example, an agreement between Belgium and Italy concerning the recognition and enforcement of judicial decisions and other enforceable instruments in civil and commercial matters of April 6, 1962 can be found at 6 Cumulative Index 146 in the Alphabetical Index, and at 6 Cumulative Index 6 in the Chronological Index. If they were to cite page 6 rather than page 146, they would <u>not</u> be demonstrating that they had found the answer by using the Alphabetical Index.

**Questions:**

1.     QUESTION:     Agreement to avoid double taxation and to prevent fiscal evasion between Finland and Israel, January 21, 1965

2.     QUESTION:     Agreement to exchange information on mental patients between the Netherlands and West Germany, July 13 and 18, 1961

3.     QUESTION:     An agreement of cultural cooperation between Poland and Mongolia, December 23, 1958

4.     QUESTION:     Agreement to permit Faroese fishermen to engage in hand line fishing off the coast of Iceland and Denmark, August 1, 1961

5.     QUESTION:     A multipartite agreement to issue to war-disabled veterans an international book of vouchers for repair of prosthetic and orthopaedic appliances, December 17, 1962

6.     QUESTION:     Transfer to the USSR of part of Finland, February 3, 1947

7.     QUESTION:     War damage claims agreement between Italy and United States, March 29, 1957

8.     QUESTION:     India and Pakistan agreement about the recovery of abducted persons, May 8, 1954

9.     QUESTION:     Agreement between Italy and Australia about the graves of Italian soldiers buried in Australia, August 27, 1953

10.     QUESTION:     Agreement to protect frontier forests against fire between Argentina and Chile, December 29, 1961

11.     QUESTION:     United States-Canadian settlement by arbitration of claims relating to Gut Dam, March 25, 1965

12.  QUESTION:  Swedish-Danish agreement about Swedish fish landings in Denmark, December 5, 1967

13.  QUESTION:  Czechoslovakia Mongolian cooperation on quarantine of plants and their protection against pests, diseases, and weeds, December 9, 1966

14.  QUESTION:  Agreement between the United Kingdom and Cameroon for interest free loan towards modernizing Cameroon's telecommunication system, June 16, 1967

15.  QUESTION:  Agreement between Canada and Bolivia on exchange of messages for third parties by amateur radio stations, May 31, 1963

16.  QUESTION:  Agreement between Canada and Italy on sale of waste materials and scrap belonging to Royal Canadian Air Force, December 18, 1961

17.  QUESTION:  Supplement of September 18, 1963 to the agreement between Canada and Italy about the sale of waste materials and scrap belonging to Royal Canadian Air Force, September 18, 1963

18.  QUESTION:  Netherlands-Germany settlement of frontier questions, April 8, 1960

19.  QUESTION:  Agreement between Romania and Yugoslavia on compensation for damages caused by the construction of the Iron Gates water power and navigation system on the Danube, November 30, 1963

20.  QUESTION:  Agreement between Netherlands and Ecuador on establishment of a dairy farming training center and modernization of technique of slaughtering cattle for consumption in Ecuador, January 14, 1965

21.  QUESTION:  Agreement between the United States and Vietnam on television broadcasting in Vietnam, January 3, 1966

22.  QUESTION:  Agreement between the United Kingdom and Greece for restoration of land on which Anglo-French Crimean War Cemetery at New Phaleron is situated, December 17, 1965-January 12, 1966

23.  QUESTION:  Service of national contingent provided by Finland with United Nations Peace-Keeping Force in Cyprus, February 21, 1966

24.  QUESTION:  Agreement between the United States and Ireland for the use of counterpart of special account for a scholarship exchange program, March 16, 1957

25.  QUESTION:  Agreement between Hungary and Iraq on cooperation in radio, television, cinema, theater, and news, October 11, 1961

# ASSIGNMENT 5

## GENERAL TREATIES

**Sources:**     *Cumulative Index. United Nations Treaty Series*
*General Index. League of Nations Treaty Series*
Parry, C., *Consolidated Treaty Series,* 1981, and
Parry, C., *Index Guide to Treaties,* based on the
Consolidated Treaty Series, General Chronological List
1648-1809.

## Method:

By using the above indexes and, when called for, consulting the treaty itself, answer the questions below. When a cite is called for, give either the *United Nations* or *League of Nations Treaty Series* volume and page number or the volume and page of treaty given in the *Consolidated Treaty Series,* for example, 364 U.N.T.S. 3, 25 L.N.T.S. 12, 1 C.T.S. 271.

Please note that the U.N.T.S. and the L.N.T.S. indexes are divided into chronological and alphabetical sections.

## Questions:

1.     QUESTION:     Where can a copy of the Capitulation of Yorktown, 1781 (Generals Washington and Cornwallis) be found?

2.     QUESTION:     Is Upper Volta a signatory to the African Migratory Locust Convention of 1962? Is Zaire?

3.     QUESTION:     Where can a copy of the Locarno Pact of 1925 (treaty of mutual guarantee final protocol) be found?

4.     QUESTION:     Is the agreement establishing the Asian Coconut Community (1968) in force? Has the Philippines ratified it?

5.     QUESTION:     Where can a copy of the Treaty of Amity, Conciliation, and Arbitration between Italy and Ethiopia (Abyssinia), 1928, be found?

6.     QUESTION:     During 1963 what nations ratified the European Convention on Academic Recognition of University Qualifications, Dec. 14, 1959?

7.     QUESTION:     Where can a copy of the agreement between the Free City of Danzig with Germany, Great Britain, Denmark, Poland, and Sweden, 1929, on the regulation of plaice and flounder fishing in the Baltic Sea be found?

8.     QUESTION:     Where can a copy of the Peace of Westphalia, 1648 (two parts), be found?

9.     QUESTION:     Cite best source for a list of the denunciations made in 1952 of the Convention for the Safety of Life at Sea, May 31, 1929

10.     QUESTION:     Where can a copy of the Tokyo Agreement of February 19, 1954 on status of U.N. forces in Japan be found?

11.     QUESTION:     Where can a copy of the Polish/Democratic Republic of Korea Cultural Cooperation Treaty of 1956 be found?

12.     QUESTION:     Where can a copy of the Mutual Assistance Treaty, Poland-Great Britain, 1939, be found?

13.     QUESTION:     Where can a copy of the Agreement Abolishing Visas, Israel-Austria, 1968, be found?

14.     QUESTION:     Where can a copy of the Treaty Between the U.S. and the Sioux Indians, 1851, be found?

15.     QUESTION:     Where can a copy of the Buraimi Oasis Arbitration Agreement of 1954 be found?

# ASSIGNMENT 6

# WHITEMAN'S DIGEST OF INTERNATIONAL LAW

**Source:**    Whiteman, Marjorie M., *Digest of International Law*
(1963-1973)

**Method:**

Use the index to Whiteman to cite the volume and page references to the
topics listed below.

**Sample answer:**      10:577

**Questions:**

| | | |
|---|---|---|
| 1. | QUESTION: | Withdrawal of Cuba from International Monetary Fund |
| 2. | QUESTION: | Dangerous or humiliating labor for prisoners of war |
| 3. | QUESTION: | Proof of nationality |
| 4. | QUESTION: | The right to blockade Suez Canal |
| 5. | QUESTION: | The legal bases of Arctic (sector principle) |
| 6. | QUESTION: | Epicontinental sea distinguished from continental shelf: superjacent waters |
| 7. | QUESTION: | Demilitarization of Aegean Sea islands |
| 8. | QUESTION: | European Commission of Human Rights |
| 9. | QUESTION: | Diplomatic status of governments-in-exile |
| 10. | QUESTION: | Estrada Doctrine |
| 11. | QUESTION: | The legality of submarine use in war |

12.    QUESTION:    Exclusion of Nazis or Facists from employment in United Nations Secretariat

13.    QUESTION:    Military air service to Berlin

14.    QUESTION:    Use of foreign flags by insurgent vessels

15.    QUESTION:    Seizure of fishing vessels in waters of contested jurisdiction off the coast of Mexico

16.    QUESTION:    List of treaties and agreements concerning refugees

17.    QUESTION:    The use of embargo as a means of reprisal

18.    QUESTION:    The passage of belligerent warships through the Turkish Straits

19.    QUESTION:    Repatriation of diplomatic officers in time of war

20.    QUESTION:    The difference between pillage and booty

21.    QUESTION:    Harvard draft convention on piracy, 1932

22.    QUESTION:    Exclusion of Cuba from OAS

23.    QUESTION:    Legal status of Enderbury Island

24.    QUESTION:    The use of Shatt-al-Arab River between Iran and Iraq by commercial vessels of all nations

25.    QUESTION:    The definition of "Hostile Propaganda"

# Chapter 22

# LEGAL RESEARCH IN THE UNITED KINGDOM

## ASSIGNMENT 1

### ENGLISH REPORTS, FULL REPRINT

**Method:**

Using the Index of Cases volumes, provide the *English Reports Full Reprint* citation for each of the cases cited.

**Questions:**

1. *In re Pugh,* 17 Beav. 336.

2. *Robinson v. Stone,* 2 Strange 1260.

3. *Smith v. Dixon,* 2 Curt. 264.

4. *Wagstaffe v. Bedford,* 1 Vern. 95.

5. *White's Case,* 6 Mod. 18.

6. *Price v. Harris,* 10 Bing. 331, 557.

7. *R. v. Nixon,* I Strange 185.

8. *Smarte v. Edsum,* 1 Lev. 30.

9. *Gibbon v. Budd,* 2 H. & C. 92.

10. *Dean v. Abel,* Dick. 287.

11. *Knox v. Brown,* 1 Eq. Rep. 126.

12. *Drew v. Coles,* 2 C. & J. 505.

13. *Buttier v. Mathews,* 19 Beav. 549.

14.     *Aarons v. Williams,* 2 Bing. 304.

15.     *Carter v. Hail,* 2 Stark 361.

16.     *Locke v. Colman,* 1 My. & Cr. 423.

17.     *Jenney v. Brook,* 6 Q.B. 323.

18.     *Lampley v. Blower,* 3 Atk. 396.

19.     *In re The Comet,* 5 C. Rob. 285.

20.     *Wilson v. Millar,* 2 Stark. 1

# ASSIGNMENT 2

## HALSBURY'S LAWS OF ENGLAND, FOURTH EDITION-- CASE METHOD

**Method:**

Locate the citation for each case, using *Halsbury's Laws of England* (4th ed.). Most cases can be found in the main volumes by using volume 54, *Consolidated Table Cases.* If more than one citation is given, cite only the first.

**Questions:**

1.  *Adley v. Whitstable Co.*

2.  *Ashworth v. Browne.*

3.  *A-G v. Prosser.*

4.  *Bandy v. Cartwright.*

5.  *Allmann v. McDaniel.*

6.  *Hodsden v. Harris.*

7.  *Guy v. Churchill.*

8.  *Dorset (Duke) v. Crosbie.*

9.  *Burg's (Lady) Case.*

10. *Herne (Lady) v. Herne.*

11. *Harman's Case.*

12. *Coleman v. North.*

13. *Ekin v. Flay.*

14. *Price v. Hall.*

15. *R. v. Noble.*

16. *Ashbee v. Pidduck.*

17.   *Clarke v. Mumford.*

18.   *The Neptune.*

19.   *The Durham City.*

20.   *Dickie v. Singh.*

# ASSIGNMENT 3

## HALBURY'S LAWS OF ENGLAND, FOURTH EDITION-- INDEX METHOD

**Method:**

Using the *Consolidated Index* volumes to the Fourth Edition of *Halsbury's Laws of England,* locate statements in the text which answer each of the following questions. Indicate where this statement was found by citing to the volume and page number of the encyclopedia.

**Questions:**

1.  Did the Highway Acts modify the common law to make it a duty of the highway authorities to light certain roads?

2.  Is there a remedy for breach of contract to marry?

3.  Can a husband be held criminally liable for the acts of his wife?

4.  Is a promoter a trustee or agent of the company he attempts to form?

5.  What is the minimum number of persons necessary to form a new company?

6.  Can money lent to an illegal company be recovered?

7.  May a person accept a revocable offer if it was not made to him?

8.  Is a contract void if one party was intoxicated when he or she entered into the contract?

9.  Is past consideration a real consideration?

10. Is taking a group picture in front of a sculpture in a museum's foyer a violation of the copyright code?

11. Is a person professing the Jewish religion disqualified from holding the position of Lord Chancellor of Great Britain?

12. May a parent be fined and even imprisoned for failure to comply with a school attendance order?

13. How many kinds of estoppel are there?

14. May a witness be asked leading questions during cross-examination in a criminal case?

15. Is it true that public statutes are judicially noticed and they need not be proved as evidence?

16. There being no special exception, may a young person be employed on Sunday?

17. May a ferry owner discriminate against certain persons as to use of his ferry?

18. Are there law on the composition and labeling of drinking milk?

19. Is there any special restriction for inventions that produce atomic energy?

20. Are clergymen exempt from jury duty?

# ASSIGNMENT 4

## HALSBBURY'S STATUTES OF ENGLAND AND WALES, FOURTH EDITION--ALPHABETICAL LIST OF STATUTES

**Method:**

Using the *Tables of Statutes* and *Index* volume of *Halsbury's Statutes* (4th ed.) to locate the text and annotations to the statute in question. Indicate, by volume and page number, where this statute can be found in this set.

**Questions:**

1.    Act of Supremacy (1558).

2.    Admiralty Pensions Act (1921).

3.    Magna Carta (1297).

4.    Caravan Sites Act 1968.

5.    Civic Amenities Act of 1967.

6.    Statute of Westminister 1931.

7.    Married Women's Property Act 1964.

8.    Union with Ireland Act 1800.

9.    Abortion Act 1967.

10.   Firearms Act 1982.

# ASSIGNMENT 5

## HALSBURY'S STATUTES OF ENGLAND AND WALES, FOURTH EDITION, INDEX METHOD

### Method:

Use the *Table of Statutes and Index* volume of *Halsbury's Statutes* (4th ed.) to find the statutory answers to the following questions. Answer the question and cite *Halsbury's Statutes* by volume and page.

### Questions:

1.    In non-emergency situations how many registered medical practitioners must approve before a pregnancy may be legally terminated?

2.    What is the maximum prison term for assaulting a clergyman?

3.    For the purpose of the law of libel and slander is the broadcasting of words by means of wireless telegraphy permanent publication?

4.    What is the maximum prison term for a second conviction for possession or sale of a flick knife?

5.    How many imcorporators are necessary in order to form a non-private company?

6.    Colossal Condominium's newest effort is on a disused burial ground. Will they be allowed to build on that location?

7.    Does the Constitution of the Board of Architectural Education permit the Cambridge University School of architecture to nominate one person to that Board?

8.    When was the Federation dissolved between Rhodesia and Nyasaland?

9.    Has the death sentence been abolished in England?

10.   Although the statutes require that the indictment for an act of treason must be processed within three years, there is one treasonous act not bound by this limitation. Name that act.

# ASSIGNMENT 6

## ENGLISH STATUTES -- *IS IT IN FORCE?*

**Method:**

Using the *Noter Up* volume which accompanies *Halsbury's Statutes,* find the following Statutes and indicate: (a) If they are currently in force, and (b) if in force, the date of receiving royal assent.

**Example:**

| | |
|---|---|
| QUESTION: | Companies Act 1976 (c69) |
| ANSWER: | (a) No. |
| | (b) Whole act repealed. |

**Questions:**

1. Chemical Weapons Act of 1996 (c6)

2. Dockyard Services Act 1986 (c52)

3. Disability Discrimination Act of 1995 (c50)

4. Sea fish Industry Act of 1973 (c29)

5. Broadcast Act 1980 (c64)

6. Trade Union Act 1984 (c49)

7. Social Security (No. 2) Act of 1980 (c39)

8. Malicious Communications Act 1988 (c27)

9. Housing (Homeless Persons) Act 1977 (c48)

10. Housing Subsidies Act 1967 (c29)

11. Mauritius Republic Act 1992 (c45)

12. Access to Medical Records Act 1988 (c28)

13. Companies Act 1980 (c22)

14.     Dangerous Wild Animals Act 1976 (c38)

15.     Southern Rhodesia Act 1979 (c52)

# ASSIGNMENT 7

# THE DIGEST - CASE METHOD

**Method:**

Locate the following case names in *Consolidated Table of Cases* volumes (2008 reissue). Using the volume number, topic name and the page or case number which you find, locate the digest of the case in question and indicate: its citation. If there is more than one citation, give only the first.

**Questions:**

1.  *Barner v. Barner* (Can.).

2.  *Bolden v. Brogden* (1838).

3   *Big Point Club v. Lozan* (Can.).

4.  *Mills v. Edwards* (1971).

5.  *Z. v. Z.* (1972)(Aus.).

6.  *R. v. Renton* 1848).

7.  *Wilson v. Grey* (1866).

8.  *Sheardown v. Good* (Can.).

9.  *Taylor v. Willoughby* (1953).

10. *Brown v. Nisbett* (1750).

11. *Gray v. Gray* (1852).

12. *The Kauss* (1904).

13. *Kearon v. Radford & Co.* (1895).

14. *Overseas Tankship v. Morts Dock* (1961).

15. *R. v. Cornwell* (1972) (Aus.).